The Traditional Greek D

It is said that if Homer were to turn up at a Greek Easter lunch party, he'd feel right at home. A lamb would be roasting on the spit, the table would be set with spring onions, lettuce, and white sheep's cheese; even the wine might have the familiar zing of resin. He would not be surprised at a family's supper during Lent either. Lentil, chickpea, or bean soup would be staples as they had been in his time, supplemented by a bowl of boiled greens dripping with olive oil and perhaps a succulent octopus or squid stew, not to mention little cakes stuffed with nuts and honey.

But while many of the basic ingredients of Greek cuisine have remained the same for millennia, it nevertheless evolved with the centuries as new techniques, fruits and vegetables, herbs and spices were introduced and assimilated. By the time the Romans took over the Mediterranean, every aristocrat wanted to employ a Greek cook. Over the years, other conquerors brought other tastes and influences, so that some Greek dishes may resemble foods found in the Arab world, the Balkans, Italy, or Turkey. Indeed, some of the most famous dishes associated with Greece – moussaka, dolmades, and eggplant Imam – came to the mainland with Greek refugees from Asia Minor.

Nevertheless, two factors can be singled out as determining the course of Greek cooking. One is simply geography: Greece is a relatively poor, mountainous country surrounded on three sides by the sea. It is a land that favors olive trees and vines, sheep and goat breeding over dairy farms and, in the coastal areas at least, plenty of seafood. Lacking natural resources, Greeks had to struggle to survive. They learned to live by their wits, saving rich meat and fish feasts for special occasions, while making game or shellfish go further by combining them with vegetables, grains, pasta, or pulses to feed large families. Meanwhile, during the Byzantine era, the all-powerful Church ruled that good Christians must fast for long periods before Christmas, Easter, Pentecost, and the Assumption of the Virgin, as well as on Wednesdays and Fridays throughout the year. Fasting meant neither subsisting on bread and water nor giving up a treat, but rather demanded that the faithful abstain from eating meat, fish, dairy products, and eggs.

Such restrictions inspired Greek housewives to ever more imaginative combinations of vegetables, with the result that Greece is one of the few countries in the world where vegetable dishes are main courses. They became masters at adding just the right herbs, wrapping leaves, stuffing vegetable cases, filling pies, and cooking everything with plenty of olive oil. Nowadays, these imaginative, nutritious dishes are what the experts point to when they tout the merits of the Mediterranean Diet.

But perhaps the most characteristic feature of any Greek meal is that it is an occasion for enjoyment and companionship. Food, for Greeks, is not just a biological need, but rather a celebration, a source of amusement and joy.

Appetizers
(Mezedes)

Fried Triangles

(Bourekakia Tiganita)

Yields 50-60 pieces • Preparation time 2 hours • Frying time 15-30 minutes

INGREDIENTS

1 package ready-made phyllo • olive or vegetable oil for frying • THE CHEESE FILLING: 1 cup milk • 3 tablespoons cream of wheat or fine semolina • 1 whole egg and 1 egg yolk, lightly beaten • 2 tablespoons melted butter • 1 cup crumbled feta cheese • 1 cup grated Swiss cheese • salt and pepper THE MEAT FILLING: 1/2 lb ground beef or veal • 2 spring onions, chopped fine • 1 small garlic clove, crushed • 1 tablespoon finely chopped dill • 1 tablespoon finely chopped parsley • 1 tablespoon olive oil • 2-3 tablespoons milk or water

Prepare the Cheese Filling: In a saucepan heat the milk with the cream of wheat, stirring constantly, and boil for a few minutes, until smooth and creamy. Remove from the heat, add the remaining ingredients, and mix well. The filling should not be runny. If it is, add more feta.

Prepare the Meat Filling: Mix all the ingredients in a small bowl. Add just enough milk or water, as needed, to make the filling moist and malleable. Carefully unfold the phyllo sheets on a flat surface. With a sharp knife cut lengthwise into strips 2 inches wide. To prevent from drying out and becoming brittle, cover the phyllo strips with a damp cloth. Place two strips one on top of the other and brush with melted butter. Put 1 teaspoon of cheese filling or meat filling in the bottom left corner and fold the right corner over it, to form a triangle. Fold the triangle over and over up the pastry strip until you reach the end. Continue with the remaining pastry and fillings until all are used up. (At this point you may freeze the triangles in plastic containers. Layer each row with wax paper. Store cheese and meat bourekakia in separate containers.) When ready to cook, deep-fry the triangles, whether frozen or freshly made, in very hot oil. Serve hot.

Baked Cheese Triangles

(Tiropitakia)

Yields 3-4 dozen • Preparation time 1 hour • Baking time 30 minutes

INGREDIENTS

2 eggs plus 1 egg yolk • 1/4 cup heavy cream • 1 lb feta cheese, crumbled • white pepper • nutmeg (optional) • 1/2 cup butter • 1/2 cup margarine • 1 lb packaged phyllo • 1 egg yolk, beaten with a little water • sesame seeds

Lightly beat the eggs with the cream in a bowl. Add cheese, pepper, and a few gratings of nutmeg. Mix well until the mixture is very thick. If necessary, add more cheese. Melt butter and margarine in a small saucepan. Lay the phyllo sheets on a flat surface and cut into strips, lengthwise, about 2½ inches wide. Brush a strip with melted butter and put another on top. Butter the surface, put 1 teaspoon of the cheese filling in the bottom left corner and fold the right corner over it, to form a triangle. Then fold the triangle over and over up the pastry strip until you reach the end. Continue with the remaining pastry and filling until both are used up. Arrange the triangles on a buttered baking tray, prick the tops with the prongs of a fork. (At this stage you may wrap the pies and freeze them. Always let them thaw out before baking.) Brush with beaten egg yolk and sprinkle with sesame seeds. Preheat oven to 400°F and bake for about 30 minutes, or until golden brown.

Meat Rolls Smyrna-Style

(Soutzoukakia Smyrneika)

Serves 4 • Preparation time 30 minutes • Cooking time 45 minutes

INGREDIENTS

• 2 thick slices bread (crusts removed) • 1/2 cup dry red wine • 1 lb ground lean meat (beef or veal) • 1/2 cup finely chopped onion • 2 garlic cloves, crushed • 1 egg • 3 tablespoons chopped parsley • 1/2 teaspoon ground cumin • salt and pepper • flour for dredging • 1/4 cup olive oil • 1/4 cup vegetable oil

THE SAUCE: 1 lb fresh tomatoes • 1 tablespoon vinegar • 1 garlic clove, chopped • 1 bay leaf • 1/2 teaspoon sugar

Soak the bread in the wine for about 5 minutes, or until thoroughly softened. Then squeeze out and reserve the excess wine. In a large bowl combine the ground meat with the wine-soaked, crumbled bread, onion, garlic, egg, parsley, cumin, and seasonings to taste. Mix the ingredients with a wooden spoon until thoroughly blended. Cover and chill for 1 to 2 hours. Moisten your hands, pinch off small portions of the meat mixture, the size of walnuts, and shape into 20 oval rolls. Roll them in flour. Heat both types of oil together in a large frying pan. Slip in the meat rolls and fry until browned all over, turning occasionally and allowing time for the meat to cook thoroughly. Remove from the pan using a slotted spoon and set aside. Strain the frying fat through a fine sieve into a cooking pan. Add all the sauce ingredients and the reserved wine. Bring to a boil and simmer until the sauce is thick. Drop in the meat rolls, stir to immerse them in the sauce, and simmer, covered, for 15 minutes. Serve hot, with rice, french fries, or mashed potatoes.

Meatballs

(Keftedakia)

Serves 4 • Preparation time 10 minutes • Cooking time 20 minutes

INGREDIENTS

2 thick slices day-old bread (crusts removed) • 1 cup finely chopped onion • 1 lb ground lean meat (beef or veal) • 1/4 cup olive oil • 1 egg • 1/4 cup chopped parsley, dill, or mint • 1 tablespoon vinegar • 1 tablespoon oregano • salt and pepper • flour for dredging • oil for frying

Soak the bread in water and squeeze out the excess with your hands. Crumble the bread and mix it with all the other ingredients in a bowl. The mixture should be moist. Add a little water or beer, if necessary. Chill the mixture, covered, for 2 hours.

Fried Keftedakia: Pinch off small pieces of the meat mixture and roll into walnut-sized balls. Dredge with flour and fry in hot olive oil until brown and crisp. Serve hot.

Grilled Keftedakia (Soutzoukakia): Add to the meat mixture 2 crushed garlic gloves and roll it into sausage-shaped rolls. Brush with oil and grill over charcoal, turning frequently, for about 15 minutes or until the meat is done to your taste. Serve hot with Tzatziki.

Keftedakia with Sauce: Prepare the fried meatballs and put them in Tomato Sauce. Cover and simmer 5-7 minutes. Serve them hot with fried potatoes or rice.

Rice-Stuffed Vine Leaves

(Dolmadakia Yialantzi)

Serves 8 • Preparation time 2 hours • Cooking time 30 minutes

INGREDIENTS

1 lb fresh or preserved vine leaves • 3 cups finely chopped spring onions • 1 lb short-grain rice • 2 cups chopped parsley • 1 cup chopped fresh dill • 2 cups olive oil • salt and pepper • 1/4 cup pine nuts (optional) • 1/4 cup currants (optional) • 1/3 cup lemon juice

Wash the vine leaves and trim the stems. Blanch them, a few at a time, in boiling water. Drain and let cool. Blanch preserved vine leaves the same way. Put the onions in a strainer, sprinkle with a little salt, and rub with your fingertips. Rinse with a little water. Squeeze out the water with your hands. Mix the rice with the onions, herbs, half the oil, seasonings to taste, pine nuts, and currants (if used). Lay the vine leaves one by one on a flat surface, shiny side down. Put about one tablespoon of the rice mixture in the lower center of a leaf, fold the sides over, and roll it up into a neat parcel. Continue stuffing the vine leaves in this way, until all the filling is used. Save any torn or damaged leaves and line the base of a large heavy-bottomed pan or flameproof casserole with them. Arrange the stuffed vine leaves on top, packing them in, seam side down, in more than one layer if necessary. Pour in the remaining oil, 2½ cups boiling water, and lemon juice. Put a heavy plate upside down on top of the stuffed vine leaves, to keep them from opening. Cover the pan and bring to a boil. Reduce the heat and simmer until all the water is absorbed, about 35-40 minutes. Let them cool in the pan and place a thick piece of paper towel or a clean dish cloth between the pan and the lid to absorb the steam. Transfer to a platter. Serve with Tzatziki or plain yogurt. Equally good served at room temperature the next day.

Grilled Sardines

(Sardeles Psites)

Serves 4 • Preparation time 30 minutes • Grilling time 8 minutes

INGREDIENTS

2 lbs fresh sardines • salt, pepper, olive oil • oregano (optional) • 2 garlic cloves, finely chopped • 1/4 cup finely chopped parsley • Oil-Lemon Dressing (page 20)

Clean the sardines and pull out the backbone carefully. It should come out easily when you pull off the head and intestines. Try not to split the fish in two. Open the sardines, rinse well, drain, and line them up on a platter. Sprinkle them with a mixture of salt, pepper, oregano, chopped garlic, and a little olive oil. Place them two together (bellies facing each other) and arrange on an oiled double grill. Brush with olive oil. Grill them over charcoal for 4 minutes on each side. Sprinkle a little more oregano over them when finished. Transfer them to a platter, sprinkle with parsley and oil-lemon dressing. Serve, garnished with slices of lemon and grilled tomatoes. An excellent accompaniment to tsipouro or ouzo.

Grilled or Fried Peppers

(Piperies Psites i Tiganites)

Serves 4 • Preparation time 10 minutes • Cooking time 10 minutes

INGREDIENTS

1 lb long green peppers • 1 chili pepper (optional) • salt to taste • Oil-Vinegar Dressing

Wash the peppers, and carefully remove the stems and seeds, taking care not to tear the peppers. Grill on charcoal or fry in a small amount of olive oil, turning them to brown all over. Arrange the peppers in a deep plate and while still hot, sprinkle them with salt and oil-vinegar dressing to taste. If you fry the peppers, do not add dressing. Spoon over 2-3 tablespoons of the frying oil, add salt and vinegar to taste. The chili pepper will give the dish a slightly hot flavor. More hot peppers can be used, if a spicier flavor is desired. Peppers served the second day are even tastier. Delicious with ouzo or retsina.

Fried Cheese

(Tiri Saganaki)

Serves 6 • Preparation time 5 minutes • Frying time 5-7 minutes

INGREDIENTS

2/3 lb kefalotiri or Romano cheese • oil for frying • 1 lemon • flour • 1/4 teaspoon pepper

Cut the cheese into 4 slices, each about 1/3 inch thick. Mix a few spoonfuls of flour and the pepper in a dish and coat the cheese slices with the mixture. Pour enough olive oil into a frying pan to cover the bottom and heat until smoking. Fry the cheese, turning once, until crisp and brown on both sides. Transfer to a platter, sprinkle with lemon juice, and serve immediately. Wonderful with ouzo.

Baked Giant or Butter Beans

(Yigantes Plaki)

Serves 4-6 • Preparation time 1 hour • Cooking time 1 hour

INGREDIENTS

1 lb dried giant or butter beans • 2 celery stalks • 1 carrot, scraped • a few peppercorns • 1 cup grated onion • 5-6 garlic cloves, slivered • 1 cup olive oil • salt and pepper • 1 teaspoon sugar • 1/2 finely chopped parsley • 2 lbs fresh or canned tomatoes • 2 large tomatoes, sliced

Soak beans in plenty of water for at least 24 hours. Drain, put in a large pan, and cover with cold water. Add the celery, carrot, and peppercorns, and bring to a boil. Reduce the heat and simmer until tender. Drain and put in a baking pan or a flameproof dish. Heat the olive oil in a saucepan, add onion and garlic, and sauté until transparent. Force the ripe tomatoes through a sieve and add to the sautéed onion. Add the sugar and seasonings to taste. Remove from the heat and stir in the parsley. Pour the sauce over the beans, and arrange the sliced tomatoes on top. Sprinkle with salt, pepper, oregano, and a little olive oil. Preheat oven to 350°F and bake for about 1 hour until all the liquid has evaporated and beans are tender. Add water if necessary while baking. Excellent hot or at room temperature.

Zucchini Fritters

(Keftedes me Kolokithakia)

Serves 4-5 • Preparation time 30 minutes • Frying time 30 minutes

INGREDIENTS

2 lbs medium zucchini • 1/4 cup grated onion • 1/4 cup olive oil • 1 cup grated kefalotiri or Romano cheese • 3/4 cup dry breadcrumbs • 3/4 cup self-raising flour • 3 eggs • 1/4 cup finely chopped dill or mint • salt, pepper • oil for frying

Wash and grate the zucchini into a colander. Sprinkle them with 1/2 teaspoon salt and let drain for an hour or so. You should have about 4 cups of grated zucchini. Meanwhile, lightly sauté the onion in the oil. Squeeze the zucchini dry, a handful at a time. In a bowl combine the zucchini with all the other ingredients, including the onion, and mix well. Heat an inch or more of oil in a large frying pan until almost smoking. Drop spoonfuls of the mixture, a few at a time, into the hot oil and fry until browned and crisp on both sides. Drain on paper towels and serve hot, accompanied by Tzatziki or Garlic Sauce.

Fish Roe Dip

(Taramosalata)

Serves 6-8 • Preparation time 15-40 minutes • In a processor 5-10 minutes

INGREDIENTS

6 thick slices dry bread, crusts removed (8 oz) • 8 oz tarama paste (salted fish roe) • 2 tablespoons minced onion • 1½ cups olive oil • 1/3 cup lemon juice • 2 spring onions, chopped • black olives to garnish

Soak the bread in a little water for 5 minutes, squeeze gently, and crumble. Pound the fish roe to a thick paste with a large mortar and pestle, if you have one. Add the onion, a few drops of the oil, and continue pounding or beating, adding a little bread along with a little oil. Continue until the bread and other ingredients are combined. Add the remaining oil little by little and then lemon juice to taste. Add it slowly to prevent curdling. Continue beating until thick and pale pink. Transfer to a serving dish, cover, and chill. Garnish with chopped green onions sprinkled on top, or with black olives. Serve with fresh country bread and ouzo.

Note: Taramosalata can be prepared in a food processor. Put the fish roe, onion, and about a third of the oil in the machine and process for a few seconds, until the red centers of the roe have been broken down and the mixture is smooth. Add the crumbled wet bread, little by little. Trickle in the remaining oil. Add the lemon juice slowly to prevent curdling and process for a few seconds until the mixture is thick and pale pink.

Alternate: Substitute 8 oz cooked potatoes for the bread. Add 2/3 cup blanched ground almonds, peanuts, or hazelnuts. If taramosalata is too thick, add a little soda water and beat until light and soft.

Shrimp in Tomato-Cheese Sauce

(Garides Saganaki me Feta)

Serves 2 • Preparation time 15 minutes • Cooking time 15 minutes

INGREDIENTS

8 large shrimps • 1/4 cup olive oil • 1/4 cup finely chopped onion • 2 cloves garlic, slivered • 1/4 cup dry white wine • 1 cup chopped fresh or canned tomatoes • 1/2 cup cubed feta cheese • 1/2 teaspoon oregano • 2 tablespoons finely chopped parsley

Peel the shrimp, leaving heads and tails intact. Heat the oil in a frying pan – in Greece, there is a special pan called a *saganaki* – and sauté the onion and garlic until translucent. Add the shrimp and fry them on both sides until they turn red. Pour in the wine and tomato and boil the shrimp, uncovered, for a few minutes, until the sauce starts to thicken. Add the cheese and oregano and stir over the heat until the cheese begins to melt into the sauce. Remove from the heat, sprinkle parsley on top, and serve immediately with plenty of country-style bread.

Walnut-Garlic Sauce

(Skordalia me Karidia)

Yields 2 cups • Preparation time 15 minutes

4 garlic cloves • 1/2 teaspoon salt • 1½ cups finely ground walnuts • 2 bread slices (crusts removed) (2 oz) • 1/2 cup olive oil • 1/4 cup vinegar

Crush garlic and salt with mortar and pestle until well blended. Add nuts gradually and blend well. Soak bread in water and squeeze it dry. Add bread, a little at a time, to the mixture and blend well. Slowly add the olive oil and the vinegar, alternately, beating well after each addition, until it resembles a smooth paste. If the mixture looks curdled, blend it slowly, adding a little warm water. Cover and chill. Serve with fried fish and vegetables.

Note: The recipe can also be prepared in a food processor or blender.

Fried Shrimp
(Garides Tiganites)

You can fry shrimp both peeled and unpeeled. When frying unpeeled shrimp, simply remove the black vein along the top by slitting the shell with a sharp knife. Wash and drain well. Dredge them in a plastic bag together with a cup or so of flour seasoned with salt and pepper. Empty them into a colander and shake to remove excess flour. Fry them in hot oil for about 4-5 minutes, but no longer or they will be too dry. For peeled shrimp, after you have removed the shell and deveined them, wash, drain, and dredge, in the same way. Dip them one at a time in egg white beaten with 1-2 tablespoons of oil and then roll them in bread crumbs. Fry them over medium heat in a deep fryer for 2-3 minutes until they become golden. Garnish with lemon rosettes, and serve with iced retsina or ouzo and Greek Village Salad.

Eggplant Salad
(Melitzanosalata)

Serves 4-8 • Preparation time 30 minutes

4 large round eggplants (2lbs) • 5-6 garlic cloves, minced • 1/4 cup vinegar • 1/3 cup olive oil • 2 teaspoons finely chopped parsley • 1 small green bell pepper, finely chopped (optional) • 1 small tomato, seeded and finely chopped (optional)

Rinse the eggplant and pat dry. Wrap each one separately in aluminum foil and grill over hot coals or on the stove, gas or electric, turning on all sides until the skin is almost completely charred. Unwrap and slit down one side lengthwise to form a boat. Arrange the eggplant boats on a platter and separate the pulp from the skin in pieces without mashing. You may empty the pulp into a serving dish. Sprinkle the pulp with salt, minced garlic, and a little parsley. Beat the vinegar with the oil until well-blended and pour into each eggplant boat. If desired, sprinkle with chopped pepper and tomato or garnish each boat with half a cherry tomato and a small garlic clove.

Octopus in Vinegar

(Ktapodi Xidato)

Serves 4-6 • Preparation time 15 minutes • Cooking time 1 hour and 30 minutes

INGREDIENTS

4 lbs octopus • 1 cup vinegar • 2 celery stalks • 2 small carrots, scrubbed • 1 medium onion, peeled • 10 peppercorns • salt

THE MARINADE: 1/3 cup olive oil • 1/3 cup vinegar • 10 peppercorns • a pinch of salt

To clean the octopus, turn the head inside out, remove and discard the viscera. Wash octopus thoroughly. Greek fishermen tenderize octopus by beating them against rocks repeatedly. You can achieve the same effect by freezing it for several days. Thaw out, place in a pot, add the vinegar and enough water to cover octopus. Bring to a boil, reduce the heat, and simmer, covered, for about 1 hour. Drain and rinse in cold water. Peel off the skin. Return to the pot, add the remaining ingredients, and water to cover. Simmer, covered, for about 30 minutes, or until tender. Drain, and cool slightly. Mix the marinade ingredients and pour the liquid over the warm octopus. Refrigerate for at least 12 hours. Garnish with pimientos and parsley. Moisten with some of the sauce and serve. Delicious with ouzo.

Charcoal-Grilled Octopus

(Ktapodi sta Karvouna)

Serves 4 • Marinating time 12 hours • Cooking time 10 minutes

2-3 lbs octopus • 1 cup vinegar

THE MARINADE: 1/2 cup olive oil • 1 cup white wine • 1 teaspoon oregano • 2 bay leaves • 10 peppercorns • salt to taste

Wash octopus and prepare according to the preceding recipe for Octopus in Vinegar. After you remove the skin, put the octopus into a bowl. Mix the marinade ingredients and pour them over the octopus. Marinate octopus up to 12 hours, in the refrigerator, turning occasionally. Just before serving, charcoal grill octopus on both sides, basting with the marinade. Serve sprinkled with olive oil and oregano and garnished with lemon wedges. Delicious with ouzo.

Peppers and Sausages in Tomato Sauce

(Spetzofai)

Serves 4 • Preparation time 2 hours • Cooking time 15 minutes

INGREDIENTS

3 lbs eggplant • 1 lb long green peppers • oil for frying • 1 lb hot, fresh pork sausages • 1/2 cup olive oil • 2 lbs fresh tomatoes, puréed

Wash, trim, and slice the eggplant into 1/2-inch thick rounds. Sprinkle generously with salt and let them stand for about 2 hours in a colander. Rinse them under running water to remove salt and squeeze out the excess water with your hands. Wash the peppers, trim off the tops, and remove the seeds. Fry the eggplant and peppers until lightly browned. Slice the sausages and brown them lightly in a skillet over medium heat. Drain and discard the fat. Replace the fat with the olive oil and finish frying. Add the tomatoes and cook for 20 minutes, until the sauce is thick. Remove the sausages with a slotted spoon and place them in an ovenproof dish. Surround with the fried eggplant and peppers, and spoon the remaining sauce over them. Sprinkle with a little freshly ground pepper, cover, preheat the oven to 350°F, and bake for about 15 minutes. Serve hot.

Mussel Pilaf with Dill

(Midopilafo me Anitho)

Serves 4 • Preparation time 50 minutes • Cooking time 25 minutes

INGREDIENTS

3 lbs fresh mussels, unshelled • 1/2 cup olive oil • 1/2 cup grated onion • 1/2 cup finely chopped spring onion • 1½ cups long-grain rice • 1/2 cup finely chopped dill • salt and freshly ground pepper

Scrub the mussels, under running water, with a stiff brush to remove seaweed and barnacles. Discard any open shells. Debeard with a sharp knife. Place the mussels in a large pan with a tiny amount of water and bring to a boil over high heat. Cover the pan and shake it from time to time, until all the mussels have opened. Discard any that do not. Strain and reserve the broth. In a clean pot, heat the oil and sauté the onions until well wilted. Add the rice and sauté, stirring, until it becomes opaque. Measure the mussel broth and add hot water to it until you have 3 cups of liquid. Bring to a boil and add it to the rice. Add salt to taste and simmer, covered, for about 20 minutes. Stir in the dill, mussels, and pepper. Place a clean cotton dish towel over the pot and replace the lid. Turn off the heat and let the rice stand for 10 minutes. Serve the pilaf hot or cold, sprinkled with a little lemon juice, some more pepper, and a little cayenne, if desired.

Steamed Mussels

(Midia Ahnista)

Serves 4 • Preparation time 45 minutes • Cooking time 5 minutes

INGREDIENTS

4 lbs live mussels • 1/2 cup olive oil • 3 tablespoons finely chopped parsley • 1 long hot green pepper, cut into rings • salt and pepper to taste • 1/4 cup lemon juice

Scrub the mussels, under running water, with a stiff brush to remove seaweed and barnacles. Discard any open shells. Place mussels in a pot of clean, salted water. They will stay alive for several hours and expel any sand or grit they contain. Change the water once or twice. Pull off the hair-like strands (beard). To open, steam them in a little water for about 2-3 minutes, and shell, reserving the liquid. Set aside. In a heavy-bottomed saucepan combine the oil, 1/2 cup of the reserved liquid, parsley, pepper rings, salt, and pepper. Bring to a rolling boil, add the mussels, and boil for 2 minutes. Remove from the heat, and stir in the lemon juice gently. Pour into a soup tureen and serve immediately. Delicious with ouzo.

Piquant Cheese Dip

(Ktipiti me Piperia)

Serves 8-10 • Preparation time 8 minutes

2 long hot green peppers • 1 lb soft feta cheese • 1/4 cup olive oil • 2-3 teaspoons vinegar to taste • 1/4 teaspoon freshly ground pepper

If the cheese is very salty, soak it in cold water for a few hours, until it is soft and lightly salted. Grill the peppers or fry them in a little hot oil. Seed and peel them. Mash the peppers and the feta with a fork, gradually adding a tablespoon of olive oil at a time, until the oil is incorporated and the mixture is smooth and soft. Add freshly ground pepper and vinegar to taste. If the mixture is stiff, add a little milk to make it creamy. If hot peppers are not available, use 2 mild peppers for the aroma and 10-15 drops of Tabasco for the bite. Serve with crackers, raw vegetables, or fresh bread.

Note: Ktipiti also can be prepared in a food processor or blender.

Salads

(Salates)

Constantinople-Style Salad

(Salata Politiki)

Serves 4 • Preparation time 30 minutes

INGREDIENTS

3 cups shredded cabbage • 3 tablespoons chopped green pepper • 3 tablespoons chopped red pepper • 4 tablespoons chopped celery • 1 large carrot, grated • Oil-Vinegar Dressing

Combine the vegetables in a large bowl. Mix well, cover, and keep refrigerated for several hours, until used. Just before serving pour the dressing over the salad and toss well.

Alternate: Add 1 cup strained yogurt to the tossed salad and mix well. Refrigerate for a few hours before serving.

Lettuce and Dill Salad

(Maroulosalata me Anitho)

Serves 4 • Preparation time 20 minutes

INGREDIENTS

1 lb romaine or other type lettuce • 5 spring onions, chopped • 2 tablespoons finely chopped fresh dill • Oil-Vinegar or Oil-Lemon Dressing

Wash the lettuce carefully and drain well. With a sharp knife cut the lettuce leaves crosswise into strips 1/3 inch wide. Try not to bruise the lettuce. Combine with the rest of ingredients in a bowl. The salad may be kept covered in the refrigerator for several hours. Just before serving toss lightly with oil-vinegar or oil-lemon dressing. Garnish with radishes, a few whole lettuce leaves, and dill.

Boiled Greens

(Horta Vrasta Salata)

Serves 4 • Preparation time 15-20 minutes

INGREDIENTS

2 lbs mixed greens (endives, dandelions, and spinach) • Oil-Lemon Dressing

Trim the greens, discarding the roots, thick stalks, and withered leaves. Wash in lots of cold water. Half fill a large kettle with water and bring to a rapid boil. Drop in the greens, cover, and bring back to the boil rapidly. Remove the cover and boil gently for 15-20 minutes, until the greens are tender. Strain well and place in a serving bowl. When ready to serve, pour oil-lemon dressing over the greens and toss lightly.

Greek Village Salad

(Horiatiki Salata)

Serves 4-6 • Preparation time 15 minutes

INGREDIENTS

2 large tomatoes • 1 cucumber • 1 medium onion, sliced • 10 black olives • 1/4 lb feta cheese, cubed (optional) • 2 hard-boiled eggs, sliced (optional) • Oil-Vinegar Dressing • parsley or watercress

Wash, dry, and cut the tomatoes in 8 wedges each. Peel and slice the cucumber. Mix the tomato and cucumber in a large bowl with the rest of the ingredients. Toss well with the oil-vinegar dressing and serve, garnished with chopped parsley or watercress sprigs.

Oil-Lemon Dressing

(Ladolemono)

Preparation time 5 minutes

2 parts olive oil • 1 part lemon juice • salt and pepper to taste • finely chopped parsley (optional)

Shake all the ingredients vigorously in a tightly-sealed jar until well blended. Use on boiled greens, vegetable salads, grilled fish, or seafood.

Oil-Vinegar Dressing

(Ladoxido)

Preparation time 5 minutes

2 parts olive oil • 1 part vinegar • salt and pepper to taste • oregano (optional) • mustard powder (optional)

Shake all the ingredients vigorously in a tightly-sealed jar until well blended. Use on any fresh vegetable salad. Add oregano or mustard powder, according to taste.

Dried Bean Salad

(Fasolia Salata)

Serves 4 • Preparation time 30 minutes • Cooking time 1 hour

INGREDIENTS

1/2 lb small dried white beans • 1 small red or Bermuda onion, sliced • 3 spring onions, chopped • 1 small green pepper, chopped • 2 tablespoons finely chopped parsley • 3 tablespoons chopped dill pickle • black olives, pitted • Oil-Vinegar Dressing

Wash and soak the beans in water overnight. Drain, place in a pan, cover with cold water, and boil for 30 minutes. Drain and return the beans to the pan. Pour enough cold water over the beans to cover and boil until tender. Drain and let cool. Place in a bowl and mix with the rest of the ingredients. Toss gently with the oil-vinegar dressing. Allow the salad to stand for a few hours before serving. Garnish with olives and serve accompanied by canned tuna fish, if desired.

Cucumber and Yogurt Dip

(Tzatziki)

Serves 6 • Preparation time 10 minutes

3 cups plain yogurt • 1 cucumber, peeled, chopped, and squeezed to remove excess liquid • 3-4 garlic cloves, crushed • 1/4 teaspoon salt • 3-4 teaspoons olive oil • 3 tablespoons finely chopped fresh dill

Line a sieve with muslin or double-thick absorbent paper towels and place the yogurt in it. Allow to drain for about 2 hours. Transfer the drained yogurt to a bowl. Stir in the cucumber, garlic, and oil. Season to taste, cover, and chill. To serve, sprinkle with chopped dill. Wonderful accompaniament for Rice-Stuffed Vine Leaves.

Soups and Sauces

(Soupes ke Saltses)

Bean Soup

(Fasolada)

Serves 6 • Preparation time 1-2 hours • Cooking time 1 hour

INGREDIENTS

1 lb dried, small white beans • 1 cup olive oil • 1 large onion, finely chopped • 1 lb fresh or canned tomatoes, peeled • 1 tablespoon tomato paste • 2 medium carrots, sliced • 1 stalk celery, sliced • 1 small green pepper, chopped • 1 small hot pepper (optional) • salt and pepper

Wash the beans well, put them in a large pan, add enough cold water to cover, and bring to a boil. Reduce the heat and simmer, covered, until soft. Do not overcook. Drain in a colander. In a heavy-bottomed pot heat the oil and sauté the onions until transparent. Purée the tomatoes in a food mill or blender and dilute the tomato paste in the purée. Add to the pot. Then add the carrots, celery, green pepper, drained beans, and seasonings. Pour in about 2 pints hot water and bring to a boil. Reduce the heat to low and simmer, covered, for 1-2 hours, or until the beans are cooked and the soup has thickened. Add more water as needed. Cooking time will depend on the freshness of the beans. Serve hot, accompanied by olives, pickled vegetables, and smoked fish.

Meat Stock

(Zomos Kreatos)

Yields 8 cups broth • Preparation time 15 minutes • Cooking time 7 hours

INGREDIENTS

2 lbs veal or beef knuckle bones • 2 lbs meaty trimmings (neck, shank, or rib tips) • 2 medium onions • 4 large carrots • 1 small celery root or 4 celery stalks • 1 leek • 4-5 parsley sprigs • 1 whole garlic • 2 cloves stuck in one of the onions • 1 bay leaf • salt

Put the meat and bones in a large, heavy, nonstick pot. Add cold water (about 6 pints) to cover. Slowly bring to a boil over medium heat and skim off the scum that rises to the top. Keep skimming, occasionally adding more cold water to delay the boiling, until no more scum appears. Add all the other ingredients and continue to skim, until the boiling point is reached. Reduce the heat and simmer slowly for 5-7 hours, occasionally skimming any scum that may appear and spooning off any excess fat from the broth surface. Strain through a very fine sieve and discard the solids. Allow stock to cool and skim fat from the surface, or refrigerate the stock and remove the solidified fat when cold. Divide the jellied stock in 1- or 2-cup portions and place in heavy plastic bags or containers. Stock will keep up to 1 week in the refrigerator and 6 months in the freezer.

Lentil Soup

(Faki Soupa)

Serves 6 • Preparation time 15 minutes • Cooking time 30 minutes to 1 hour

INGREDIENTS

1 lb lentils • 1½ cups puréed fresh or canned tomatoes • 1 cup oil • 2 small whole onions • 5 whole garlic cloves • 2 tablespoons vinegar • 1/2 teaspoon sugar • salt and pepper to taste • 2 bay leaves (optional) • 1/2 teaspoon oregano (optional)

Wash and pick over the lentils. Put all the ingredients except the lentils in a large pot with 2 pints of water. Add all ingredients except for the lentils. Bring to a boil. Add the lentils, cover, and simmer for about 30 minutes to 1 hour, depending on the quality of lentils, until they are tender and the soup is thick. Add some more water if necessary. Some people remove and discard the onions, garlic, and bay leaves before serving. Others find the first two delicious. Serve hot or cold, sprinkled with freshly ground pepper and accompanied by olives, and smoked trout.

Chick-Pea Soup

(Revithosoupa or Revithada)

Serves 6 • Preparation time 12 hours • Cooking time 1 hour and 30 minutes

INGREDIENTS

1 lb chick-peas • 1 tablespoon baking soda • 2/3 cup olive oil
2 small whole onions • salt and pepper to taste

Wash chick-peas and let soak overnight in warm water with the baking soda. Next day drain and rinse thoroughly. Place the peas in a large pot with cold water to cover. Slowly bring to a boil, removing the scum that rises to the top. Pour in the oil, add the onions, and simmer, covered, until the chick-peas are tender and the liquid has reduced to the desired consistency. Add a little hot water, if necessary. Remove the onions with a slotted spoon and discard or, if desired, mash one of them and return it to the soup, stirring well. Add salt to taste and cook for about 15 more minutes. Serve hot, sprinkled with freshly ground pepper and accompanied by olives.

Chicken Soup with Egg-Lemon Sauce

(Kotosoupa Avgolemono)

Serves 4-5 • Preparation time 15 minutes • Cooking time 1 hour

INGREDIENTS

1 whole chicken • 1/4 cup butter or margarine • 1 small carrot (optional) • 1 small onion (optional) • salt and pepper • 1/2 cup short-grain rice • 1 egg • 1/3 cup lemon juice • freshly ground pepper

Take the skin off the chicken and discard. Wash the chicken inside and out under cold running water. Place in a large pot. Pour in enough water to cover the chicken. Slowly bring to a boil, skimming off the scum from the top. Add the butter, carrot, onion, salt, and pepper. Cover and simmer until the chicken is tender. Remove the chicken and vegetables and strain the broth into a clean pot. Bring the strained broth back to the boil, add rice, and stir well. Cover, reduce the heat, and simmer for about 20 minutes until the rice is tender. Lightly beat the egg in a bowl and add the lemon juice, a little at a time, beating continuously. Gradually pour 5-6 tablespoons of the hot soup into the egg mixture, beating all the time. Pour the egg-lemon sauce back into the soup, stirring constantly. Remove from the heat immediately to prevent curdling. Sprinkle the soup with freshly ground pepper and serve hot, accompanied by the chicken which may be either hot or cold. Serve the chicken with mayonnaise or tartar sauce.

Meatball Soup with Egg-Lemon Sauce

(Yiouvarlakia Avgolemono)

Serves 4-6 • Preparation time 30 minutes • Cooking time 30 minutes

INGREDIENTS

1 lb ground meat • 1 small onion, finely chopped • 1/4 cup short-grain rice • 3 tablespoons finely chopped parsley • 2 tablespoons finely chopped dill or mint • 2 tablespoons olive oil • salt and pepper • flour for dredging • 5 cups beef stock or water • 1/4 cup butter or margarine • 2 eggs • 1/4 cup lemon juice

In a large bowl, combine the ground meat, chopped onion, rice, herbs, olive oil, and seasonings. Knead for a few minutes, shape the mixture into small balls, and roll them in flour. Set aside. Pour the beef stock or water in a large saucepan, add the butter, and bring to a boil. Gently lower in the meat balls, a handful at a time. Don't add them all at once or the temperature will drop. Reduce the heat and simmer, covered, for about 30 minutes, until the meat is cooked. Meanwhile, lightly beat the eggs in a bowl. Add the lemon juice a little at a time, beating continuously. Then, still beating, ladle in some of the hot broth from the saucepan. Stirring vigorously, add the warm egg-lemon mixture to the soup. Immediately remove the saucepan from the heat and serve.

Fish Soup
(Psarosoupa)

Serves 6 • Preparation time 1 hour • Cooking time 1 hour and 10 minutes

INGREDIENTS

3 lbs fish (cod, grouper, or other soup fish) • 6 large carrots • 1 celery stalk • 1 leek • 1 small whole onion • 1 large green bell pepper • 3 small zucchini • 4 large potatoes, quartered • 2/3 cup olive oil • 15 peppercorns • 1/3 cup lemon juice • salt and freshly ground pepper

Trim and wash the vegetables. Place all the vegetables in a large pot, except for the potatoes. Add 2 pints of water together with the olive oil, peppercorns, and salt, and bring to a boil. Reduce the heat and simmer for 30 minutes. In the meantime, clean and wash the fish. Cut it in half, if too large for the pot. With a slotted spoon remove the vegetables, reserving the celery, zucchini, and carrots. Place the fish in the broth, bring to a boil, reduce the heat, and simmer for 10-15 minutes. Try not to overcook the fish. Remove the fish to a platter and strain the broth through a fine sieve into a clean pot. Bring back to the boil, add the potatoes and simmer until done, approximately 20 minutes. Mash one or two potatoes and stir into the broth to thicken it. Coarsely chop the carrots, celery, and zucchini and add them to the broth. When the soup returns to the boil, remove it from the heat, stir in the lemon juice, and sprinkle with freshly ground pepper. Serve hot, accompanied by the fish, either plain or garnished with mayonnaise, capers, and sliced pickles.

Easter Soup with Lamb

(Mageiritsa me Arnaki)

Serves 6-8 • Preparation time 1 hour • Cooking time 40 minutes

INGREDIENTS

1½ lb lean lamb, boned • 1/3 cup olive oil • 16 spring onions, finely chopped • 1/2 cup finely chopped dill • 1/2 cup finely chopped parsley • salt and freshly ground pepper • 1/2 cup Carolina rice • 2 eggs • 1/2 cup lemon juice

Boil the meat in a pot with ample water to cover, skimming off the foam as it rises, until the meat is very tender, about 1 hour. Remove it from the broth and cut into smallish cubes. Refrigerate the broth and remove the solidified fat when cold. Measure the broth and add water if necessary so that you have 12 cups of liquid. Put it in a large pot and bring to a boil. When the broth starts to bubble, add the cubed meat, oil, spring onions, herbs, and seasonings. Cover and simmer for 20 minutes until the onions are soft. Rinse the rice in plenty of cold water, drain, and add it to the broth. Let the soup simmer for another 20 minutes, until the rice is cooked. In the meantime, lightly beat the eggs in a bowl, pour in the lemon juice, and beating all the while, gradually add a few tablespoons of the hot broth. Pour the sauce back into the soup, stirring vigorously, and remove it from the heat. This is a wonderful, light variation on the classic Easter soup. Serve hot.

Savory Pies

(Pites)

Ground Meat Pie

(Kreatopita me kima)

Yields 20-24 pieces • Preparation time 2 hours • Baking time 1 hour

INGREDIENTS

1 recipe, Homemade Phyllo Dough • 1 1/3 cups olive oil • THE FILLING: 1 cup grated onion • 2 small leeks, chopped • 1/3 cup butter • 1 lb ground lean meat (beef or veal) • 1/4 cup olive oil • salt and pepper • 1 cup beef stock • 1/2 cup finely chopped dill • 5 eggs, lightly beaten • 1/2 cup light cream • 1 cup grated feta cheese

Prepare the phyllo dough, divide into 12 balls, cover with a damp cloth, and set aside. Heat the butter in a saucepan and sauté the meat, onions, and leeks. Add the beef stock, salt and pepper, cover, and simmer, until the meat is tender and juices have evaporated. Remove from the heat and fold in the eggs and cream. Add the dill and set aside. Roll out the dough balls into 6-inch circles. Brush circles generously with butter. Stack 5, one on top of the other, and roll out into a rather thick sheet. Repeat with another 5 stacked circles. Roll the remaining 2 circles, individually, into very thin circles. Grease a round (14-inch) baking pan, line it with one 5-layer sheet, brush with butter. Place a single sheet over it and brush generously with butter. Spread the meat mixture evenly on top, sprinkle with the grated feta cheese, and cover with the remaining single sheet. Brush with butter and top with the other 5-layer sheet. Moisten edges, press firmly together, and crimp. Score the pie in serving pieces and brush the top with the remaining butter. At this point either wrap and freeze, or preheat oven to 350°F and bake for about 1 hour, until golden brown. Serve hot.

Alternate: The pie may also be made with puff pastry (in this case do not use any butter) or with packaged phyllo, which requires less melted butter than homemade dough.

Mixed Greens Pie

(Hortopita)

Yields 20 pieces • Preparation time 1 hour • Baking time 1 hour

INGREDIENTS

2 lbs fresh or frozen greens (spinach, dandelions, endives) • 1/3 cup olive oil • 3/4 cup grated onion • 8 fresh spring onions, finely chopped • 1 leek, finely chopped (optional) • 1/2 cup finely chopped dill • 1/2 cup finely chopped parsley • salt and pepper • 1 lb packaged phyllo • 3/4 cup oil (half olive, half vegetable) • 1/2 cup club soda (carbonated water)

Wash and finely chop the greens. Sprinkle with a little salt and rub with your hands until they wilt. Squeeze out all the water. If using frozen greens, just squeeze out the water. Heat the oil in a saucepan and sauté the onions and leek over high heat. Add the greens, dill, parsley, salt, and pepper, stir, and remove from the heat. Line a buttered baking pan with half the phyllo sheets, one on top of the other, brushing each one with oil. Spread the filling evenly on top and cover with the remaining phyllo sheets, brushing each with oil. Score the pie into serving pieces, and brush the surface with the remaining oil. Preheat oven to 400°F and bake for 15 minutes, remove from the oven, and sprinkle with club soda. Replace the pan in the oven and continue baking for approximately 45 minutes or until golden brown. Serve hot or cold.

Zucchini Cheese Pie

(Kolokithotiropita)

Yields 20-24 pieces • Preparation time 2 hours • Baking time 1 hour

INGREDIENTS

1 recipe, Home-made Phyllo Dough • 2/3 cup olive oil • 2/3 cup margarine

THE FILLING: 2 lbs zucchini, grated • 1 lb feta cheese, crumbled • 5-6 eggs • 3 tablespoons cream of wheat or semolina • 3 tablespoons melted butter • 1/2 cup heavy cream or evaporated milk • 1/2 cup teaspoon freshly ground pepper • 1/2 teaspoon cinnamon • 1/2 teaspoon sugar • 1/2 cup finely chopped parsley or dill

Prepare home-made phyllo dough and divide into 12 balls. Cover with a damp towel, and allow to rest for 1 hour. Sprinkle the grated zucchini with 1/2 teaspoon salt, rub slightly with your hands, and leave to drain in a colander. Mix the zucchini with all the other filling ingredients in a bowl. Set aside. In a small saucepan, melt the margarine combined with the olive oil. On a floured pastry board roll out the 12 balls, one by one, into very thin sheets, just before baking. Line the bottom of a buttered baking pan (12x14 inches), with 5 phyllo sheets, one on top of the other, brushing each one with the oil and margarine mixture. Spread half the filling mixture over them. Cover with 2 buttered phyllo sheets. Spread them with the rest of the filling. Cover with the remaining phyllo, brushing again with butter. Press edges firmly together and crimp. Score the pie in serving pieces and brush top with remaining oil-margarine mixture. Sprinkle with a little water, preheat oven to 350°F, and bake until golden brown, approximately 1 hour.

Alternate: If using ready-made phyllo, buy 1 package. Butter the sheets lightly. Use 1/2 cup olive oil and 1/2 cup margarine. After scoring the pie, brush with the remaining oil and margarine mixture, mixed with 4 tablespoons flour and enough water (about 1 cup), to form a smooth light batter. This will thicken the paper-like texture of ready-made phyllo. Bake as above.

Leek and Cheese Pie

(Prassotiropita)

Yields 20-24 pieces • Preparation time 1 hour and 30 minutes • Baking time 50 minutes

INGREDIENTS

1 lb ready-made phyllo dough sheets or • 1 recipe, Home-made Phyllo Dough • 2 lbs leeks, chopped • 1 cup evaporated milk • 1/4 cup chopped parsley or mint • 1/4 cup melted butter • 1 lb feta cheese, crumbled • 6 eggs, lightly beaten • salt and pepper to taste • 1 tablespoon fine bread crumbs • 1/2 cup melted margarine • 1/2 cup olive oil

Divide the dough into 12 balls and roll out according to the recipe for Ground Meat Pie. Blanch the leeks and drain. Put them in a saucepan with the milk and simmer, covered, until the leeks are tender and the sauce is thick. Remove from the heat, add parsley, butter, cheese, and season to taste. Fold in the eggs. Line a large oiled round (14-inch) baking pan with one (5-layer) phyllo sheet and brush with butter. Place a single sheet over it, brush with butter, sprinkle with bread crumbs, and spread the leek filling evenly on top. Cover with the remaining single sheet, brush with butter, and top with the second 5-layer phyllo sheet. Moisten edges, press firmly together, and crimp. Score the pie into serving pieces, and brush the surface with the remaining butter. (At this point, you may wrap and freeze the pie. When ready to bake, let it thaw out first.) Sprinkle the top with a little water, preheat oven to 350°F, and bake for 40-50 minutes, until golden brown. Serve hot or cold.

Alternate: Use 1 lb leeks and 1 lb spinach.

Note: If using ready-made phyllo, place half the sheets on the bottom of baking pan and the other half on top of the filling. Brush each sheet with melted butter. Ready-made phyllo dough does not absorb as much butter as homemade.

Cheese Pie

(Tiropita)

Yields 20-24 pieces • Preparation time 1 hour • Baking time 50 minutes

INGREDIENTS

1 lb packaged phyllo • 1 lb feta cheese, crumbled • 1 cup light Béchamel • 4 eggs, lightly beaten • pepper • nutmeg • 1 tablespoon grated onion • 3/4 cup butter or margarine, melted

Prepare the béchamel, remove from the heat, and stir in pepper, nutmeg, and grated onion. Add the eggs and feta cheese. Mix well. Line a buttered baking pan (12x14 inches) with half the phyllo sheets, one on top of the other, brushing each one with melted butter. Spread the cheese mixture on top and cover with the remaining phyllo, brushing again with butter. Score the top sheets into squares and brush with the remaining butter. (At this stage you may freeze the pie. When ready to bake, let it thaw out first.) Sprinkle with 2 or 3 tablespoons water. Preheat oven to 350°F and bake for 40-50 minutes, until golden brown. Serve hot.

Béchamel (White Sauce)

(Aspri Saltsa)

Yields 1 cup • Preparation time 5 minutes • Cooking time 15 minutes

LIGHT SAUCE

1 cup milk • 2 tablespoons all-purpose flour • 2 tablespoons butter • salt and white pepper • nutmeg

THICK SAUCE

1 cup milk • 3 tablespoonsall-purpose flour • 3 tablespoons butter • salt and white pepper • nutmeg

Heat the milk in a small pot. Melt the butter in a heavy-bottomed saucepan. Stir in the flour and sauté 2-3 minutes. Off the heat, pour in the hot milk, stirring constantly with a wire whisk to blend the mixture. Return to the heat and simmer until thick. To remove any lumps, strain the sauce through a sieve placed over another pan. Return the strained sauce to the heat and simmer for about 15 minutes, whisking constantly to prevent the sauce from sticking to the bottom of the pan. Remove from the heat. Season with salt, white pepper, and a pinch of nutmeg.

Sweet Pumpkin Pie

(Kolokithopita Glikia)

Yields 20-24 pieces • Preparation time 1 hour and 30 minutes • Baking time 1 hour

INGREDIENTS

1 lb packaged phyllo • 2 lbs pumpkin • 2/3 cup sugar • 1 tablespoon semolina • 6 eggs, lightly beaten • 1/2 cup heavy cream • 1½ teaspoon cinnamon • 1/4 teaspoon nutmeg • 1 cup melted butter or margarine

Peel, deseed squash, and cut in pieces. Steam or boil in a little water until tender. Drain and mash. Put in a bowl with the sugar, eggs, cream, and spices. Set aside. Brush one half of each phyllo sheet with the melted butter, fold the other half over it, and butter the surface. Spread 2-3 tablespoons of the filling lengthwise and roll up the phyllo. Twist the roll into a coil in the center of a buttered, round (14-inch) baking pan. Repeat with the remaining sheets, twisting the rolls around the center coil. Brush top with butter, sprinkle with water, preheat oven to 350°F, and bake until golden (about 1 hour). Serve hot or cold, sprinkled with cinnamon, and powdered sugar.

Home-made Phyllo Dough

(Zimi gia Phyllo)

Yields about 1 lb • Preparation time 30 minutes

1 lb all-purpose flour • 2 tablespoons oil • 1 tablespoon vinegar • 2 teaspoons salt • 2 teaspoons baking powder (optional) • 1 cup lukewarm water

Sift the flour into a medium bowl. Make a well in the center. Pour the oil, vinegar, baking powder, salt, and water into the well. Using your hands, gradually draw the flour into the center. Knead until you have a soft, elastic dough. Add more water, if necessary. Divide the dough into small balls, according to the number of phyllo sheets you desire. Place them in a floured pan, next to each other, covered with a damp cloth. Let the dough rest for an hour or two. Flatten each ball with a rolling pin, on a floured board, and roll until very thin. To get the dough extra thin, roll each phyllo sheet around the rolling pin, pressing lightly and rolling backwards and forwards, until it is about 1/8 inch thick or thinner. To prevent the dough from sticking, sprinkle a little flour on the surface of the sheet frequently.

Cooked Vegetables

(Ladera)

Onion-Stuffed Eggplant

(Melitzanes Imam)

Serves 4-5 • Preparation time 1 hour and 30 minutes • Cooking time 1 hour

INGREDIENTS

8 medium eggplants (3 lbs) • 4 large onions, quartered • 8 garlic cloves, sliced • 1 cup olive oil • 1¾ cups puréed fresh or canned tomatoes • 1/2 cup finely chopped parsley • salt and pepper

Wash the eggplant and lop off the tops and bottoms. Pare them lengthwise in strips, leaving about an inch of skin in between. Using a sharp knife, make two incisions lengthwise in each eggplant, making sure not to cut all the way to the end. Sprinkle the eggplant with plenty of salt and set aside for 1-2 hours in a colander. Rinse under running water, squeeze out excess liquid with your hands, and pat dry. Heat half the oil in a frying pan and sauté the eggplant a few at a time, turning them several times, until lightly browned all over. Transfer to a baking pan, side by side. Sauté the onions and garlic in the hot oil, for about 5 minutes, until transparent. Add the tomatoes, parsley, and seasonings. Cook for about 10 minutes. To stuff the eggplant, spoon the mixture between the incisions, pressing it in with your fingers or the back of a spoon. Pour any remaining sauce over the eggplant. Drizzle the remaining fresh oil on top, sprinkle with a few gratings of pepper, preheat oven to 350°F, and bake for about 1 hour. Add a little water if the dish seems too dry. Serve hot or cold.

Baked Mixed Vegetables

(Briami)

Serves 6 • Preparation time 1 hour and 30 minutes • Cooking time 40 minutes

INGREDIENTS

1 lb eggplant • 1 lb zucchini • 1/2 lb fresh green beans, stringed and cut in thirds • 2 large potatoes, peeled and cut in large chunks • 2 large carrots, peeled and cut in chunks • 2 medium green bell peppers, seeded and sliced • 6-8 large fresh mushrooms, wiped clean and quartered • 2 lbs fresh ripe tomatoes, chopped • 1/2 cup olive oil • 2 medium onions, sliced • salt and pepper • 2-3 garlic cloves, sliced (optional) • 1/2 cup chopped parsley • 1/2 cup grated kefalotiri or Romano cheese • oil for frying

Wash and trim the eggplant and zucchini. Cut them in large chunks. Salt both generously and let stand in separate colanders for about 1-2 hours. Rinse in plenty of water and squeeze out excess. Heat half the olive oil and fry them, lightly. Set aside. In the same pan sauté the beans, potatoes, carrots, peppers, and mushrooms lightly in hot oil. Set aside. Heat the rest of the oil in a deeper saucepan and sauté the onions and garlic. Add the tomatoes and simmer for about 10 minutes. Add the parsley and seasonings, stir well, and remove the pan from the heat. Put all the fried vegetables into a large clay or ovenproof dish and toss gently. Pour the sauce over the dish and cover with aluminum foil. Preheat the oven to 350°F and bake for about 40 minutes. Remove the foil, sprinkle the top with grated cheese, and brown for about 10 minutes more. Serve hot or cold.

Rice-Stuffed Tomatoes and Peppers

(Domatopiperies Yemistes)

Serves 6 • Preparation time 1 hour • Cooking time 1 hour and 40 minutes

INGREDIENTS

6 large tomatoes • 6 large green bell peppers • 2 tablespoons ketchup • 2 tablespoons tomato paste • 1¼ cups short-grain rice • 1¼ cups olive oil • 1 cup grated onion • salt and pepper • 2/3 cup finely chopped parsley • 2 tablespoons minced mint (optional) • 4 large potatoes

Choose firm round tomatoes and peppers. Wash and wipe dry. Slice off the stem ends of the tomatoes and carefully scoop out most of the pulp, leaving only a thin layer next to the skin. Slice off pepper tops, leaving the stalks intact, and remove the seeds. Reserve both sets of tops. Set aside. Purée the tomato pulp and mix with the ketchup and tomato paste. Wash the rice in a strainer until the water runs clear. Set aside. Heat half the oil in a saucepan, add the onion, and sauté until transparent. Pour in 2/3 of the tomato purée, add seasonings, and boil for 10 minutes, over medium heat. Remove from the heat. Add the rice, parsley, and mint. Mix well. Loosely stuff the tomatoes and peppers two-thirds full with the rice mixture. Pack them close together in a shallow baking pan. Replace the tops of each tomato and pepper. Peel and cut the potatoes into eighths and place them between the stuffed vegetables. Pour the remaining tomato purée over the potatoes, and sprinkle with a little salt and pepper. Spoon the rest of the oil over the stuffed vegetables and potatoes. Preheat oven to 350°F and bake for about 1 hour and 40 minutes. Add a little water, if necessary, while baking. Serve hot or cold.

Braised Green Beans

(Fasolakia Yiachni)

Serves 5-6 • Preparation time 45 minutes • Cooking time 1 hour

INGREDIENTS

3 lbs fresh or 2 lbs frozen green beans • 1 cup olive oil • 1 small onion, grated • 4 spring onions, finely chopped • 3 garlic cloves, sliced • 1½ cups chopped fresh or canned tomatoes • 1/2 cup finely chopped parsley • 1/2 teaspoon sugar • salt and pepper

String the beans and cut off the tips. Wash in cold water and drain. Snap the beans in half, slice lengthwise, or leave whole. Heat the oil in a large pan and gently sauté the onions and garlic until soft but not brown. Add the tomatoes and sauté for a few more minutes over high heat. Add the beans and the remaining ingredients. Pour 1/2 cup water over them and stir well. Simmer, covered, for about 1 hour, or until the beans are tender and the sauce is thick. Serve the beans hot or cold, accompanied by Tzatziki or Beet Salad with Garlic Sauce.

Braised Okra

(Bamies Yiachni)

Serves 4 • Preparation time 30-40 minutes • Cooking time 15 minutes

INGREDIENTS

• 1 lb fresh or frozen okra • vinegar or lemon juice • 3/4 cup olive oil • 1 medium onion, grated • 1 lb fresh or canned tomatoes, puréed • 6 tablespoons finely chopped parsley • 1/8 teaspoon sugar • salt and pepper • 3 lemon slices, peeled • 1 ripe tomato, sliced

Wash fresh okra and carefully trim the cone-shaped stem ends, taking care not to pierce them. Dip trimmed tops in salt. Leave the okra to stand in a colander for a half hour. Frozen okra need no trimming. Rinse fresh or frozen okra with water and a little vinegar or lemon juice. Heat the oil in a shallow pan, add the onion, and sauté until transparent. Add tomatoes, parsley, sugar, and pepper. Cover, and simmer for 10 minutes. Add okra, and lemon slices. Stir gently into the sauce, and arrange the tomato slices on top, sprinkled with a little salt and pepper. Cover and bring to a boil over medium heat. Reduce heat and simmer for about 15 minutes. Do not overcook. Add water only if the dish seems dry. Correct seasonings but do not stir the okra while they are cooking, as they are delicate; just shake the pot a few times. Serve the dish hot or cold, it is just as tasty. Feta cheese or Piquant Cheese Dip is a perfect accompaniment.

Artichokes Constantinople-Style

(Anginares Politikes i a la Polita)

Serves 4 • Preparation time 30 minutes • Cooking time 30 minutes

INGREDIENTS

8 fresh or frozen artichokes • 1 cup olive oil • 1 medium onion, grated • 4 fresh spring onions, chopped • 2 large carrots, sliced • 3 large potatoes, cut in quarters • 1/4 lb frozen peas (optional) • 1/2 cup finely chopped dill • salt and pepper • 1 egg • 1/4 cup lemon juice

If using fresh artichokes, wash them well. Cut off the stem and peel off the dark green outer leaves. Depending on the tenderness of the leaves, remove 1/3 to 2/3 of each artichoke and cut off the tops, about an inch or two from the bottom. Scrape out the fuzzy choke from the center with a teaspoon. Rub each artichoke heart with lemon and place in a bowl with some water, a little flour, and lemon juice to prevent discoloring. Gently heat the oil in a shallow pan and sauté the onions. Add carrots and sauté lightly. Arrange the artichokes in the pan, add the potatoes, peas, dill, seasonings, and 1 cup hot water. Cover and simmer for about 30 minutes until the artichokes and potatoes are tender and the sauce is reduced. Add some more water during the cooking time, if necessary. Beat the egg with lemon juice in a bowl. Slowly add a few tablespoons of the pan juices, beating continuously, and pour the sauce back into the pan. Shake the pan to incorporate the egg and lemon sauce.

Alternate: Plain lemon juice may be substituted for the egg and lemon sauce. Serve hot or cold.

Meats

(Kreata)

Lamb Parcels

(Arni Kleftiko)

Serves 6 • Preparation time 1 hour • Baking time 50 minutes

INGREDIENTS

2 lbs boneless lamb, cut in small cubes • salt, pepper, and oregano • 2 tablespoons lemon juice • 2-3 tablespoons olive oil plus 1/3 cup • 1/2 lb frozen peas • 3 medium carrots, sliced • 3 tablespoons butter, clarified • 2 garlic cloves, sliced • 3 large potatoes, diced • 2 large tomatoes, each cut in 6 slices • 6 phyllo sheets • oil for brushing • 1/2 lb kefalotiri or pecorino cheese, diced

Season the meat lightly with pepper and oregano. Toss with lemon juice and oil to coat. Cover and marinate for 1-2 hours in the refrigerator. Meanwhile, blanch the peas and carrots in lightly salted water for 5 minutes and drain. Heat the oil in a heavy-bottomed saucepan. Add the meat cubes and sauté until lightly browned all over. Add the garlic, season lightly with salt, and set aside. Half fry the potatoes in a fryer and allow to drain on paper towels. Heat a small amount of oil in a large skillet and fry the tomato slices on both sides. Brush the top half of each phyllo sheet with oil and fold the other half over it. Brush again with oil. Do the same with the other phyllo sheets and distribute the lamb pieces, vegetables, and cheese evenly among them. Top with 2 slices of tomato and sprinkle with oregano and freshly ground pepper. Do not add salt, as the cheese is quite salty. Wrap and tie the phyllo with thick cotton string as if making 6 beggar's purses. Preheat oven to 350°F, place in a roasting pan, and bake for about 50 minutes. Serve immediately accompanied by Lettuce and Dill Salad.

Baked Lamb with Orzo

(Arni Yiouvetsi)

Serves 6 • Preparation time 30 minutes • Cooking time 2 hours

INGREDIENTS

1/2 cup olive oil • 3 lbs stewing lamb, cut into portions • 3 cups puréed fresh or canned tomatoes • 4 garlic cloves, sliced • 1/2 teaspoon sugar • salt and pepper • 1/2 cup margarine or butter • 1 lb orzo • 1/2 cup grated kefalotiri or Romano cheese, plus more for the table

Heat the oil in a large heavy-bottomed pan. Add the lamb and lightly brown the pieces all over. Add the tomatoes, garlic, sugar, and seasonings to taste. Cover and simmer for 1 hour. Meanwhile, heat the butter in a frying pan and sauté the orzo for a few minutes over high heat, until golden. Transfer to an ovenproof dish. In Greece a special clay pot called "yiouvetsi" is used. Six individual glass or glazed ceramic pots could also be used. Arrange the lamb portions on the orzo and pour the sauce over them. Add 3 cups of hot water and cover the dish. Preheat the oven to 350°F and bake for 1 hour, or until all the water has been absorbed and the pasta is soft. Add extra hot water, if necessary, if the dish seems too dry. Fifteen minutes before it is completely cooked, remove the lid and sprinkle with the grated cheese. Continue to bake, uncovered, until the cheese has melted and is lightly browned. Serve hot with additional grated cheese.

Alternate: The lamb in this recipe can be replaced by veal or other tender meat.

Moussaka

(Moussakas)

Serves 8-10 • Preparation time 2 hours • Cooking time 35-40 minutes

INGREDIENTS

5 lbs round eggplant • 1/3 cup olive oil • 1 large onion, grated • 2 garlic cloves, sliced • 1½ lbs ground lean meat (beef or veal) • 3 cups puréed fresh or canned tomatoes • 1/2 teaspoon sugar • salt and pepper • 2 egg whites, lightly beaten • 1/2 cup finely chopped parsley • 6 tablespoons fine bread crumbs • 3 cups thick Béchamel • 1/2 cup heavy cream • 3 eggs, lightly beaten • 1 cup grated kefalotiri or Romano cheese

Wash and trim the eggplant. Slice into 1/2-inch thick rounds. Sprinkle generously with salt and leave them to drain in a colander for 2 hours. Rinse, squeeze gently, and pat them dry with paper towels. Fry in hot oil until lightly browned on both sides. Drain and set aside. Heat the oil in a heavy-bottomed saucepan and sauté the onion and garlic until transparent. Add the meat and stir for 10 minutes until it begins to brown. Add the tomatoes and the sugar, and season to taste. Simmer, covered, until all the liquid evaporates. Allow to cool, and mix in the lightly-beaten egg whites and the chopped parsley. Sprinkle the bottom of a 12x14-inch buttered ovenproof dish with 2 tablespoons bread crumbs, arrange half the eggplant slices in a layer on top, and spread half the meat sauce over the eggplant. Sprinkle with half the grated cheese and 2 more tablespoons of bread crumbs. Cover with the remaining eggplant, the remaining meat sauce, and sprinkle the top with the rest of the grated cheese and the remaining bread crumbs. (At this stage you may freeze the dish, covered tightly. When ready to bake, let it thaw out first.) Prepare 3 cups thick béchamel sauce, stir in the cream and eggs. Preheat the oven to 400°F, pour the sauce over the moussaka, and bake for about 45 minutes until nicely browned. Let the dish stand for 15 minutes before serving. Serve with Greek Village Salad.

Alternate: Replace half or all the eggplant with sliced potatoes, or substitute zucchini for the eggplant. A combination of eggplant, zucchini, and potatoes can also be used.

Baked Pasta

(Pastitsio)

Serves 8-10 • Preparation time 1 hour • Baking time 1 hour

INGREDIENTS

1/2 cup olive oil • 1 medium onion, chopped • 2 lbs ground meat (beef or veal) • 2 cups puréed fresh or canned tomatoes • 1 tablespoon tomato paste • 1/2 teaspoon sugar • 3 tablespoons finely chopped parsley • salt and pepper • 1 egg, lightly beaten • 1 lb ziti or thick spaghetti • 1/4 cup melted butter • 2½ cups grated cheese (Swiss, Gouda, or Cheddar) • 2 tablespoons fine bread crumbs • 4 cups thick Béchamel • 4 eggs, lightly beaten • nutmeg

Heat the oil in a saucepan and sauté the onion until transparent. Stir in ground meat and sauté 10-15 minutes until slightly browned. Mix the tomato purée, tomato paste, sugar, and parsley, and pour it over the meat. Cover and simmer until all the liquid is absorbed. Remove from the heat, and allow to cool 5 minutes. Fold in the egg and 1/2 cup of the grated cheeses. Taste and season with salt and pepper. Set aside. Boil the pasta in lightly salted water until tender. Strain and toss with melted butter. When cool, mix in remaining cheeses, and set aside. Prepare 4 cups thick béchamel and fold in the 4 lightly-beaten eggs. Add salt, pepper, and a pinch of nutmeg. Butter an ovenproof dish (12x14 inches), sprinkle the bottom with fine bread crumbs, and spread half the pasta over them. Place the meat mixture on top and cover with the remaining pasta. Pour the béchamel over the dish, preheat the oven to 350°F, and bake for about 1 hour, until golden brown. Allow the dish to stand 10 minutes, then cut into portions, and serve hot accompanied by Greek Village Salad.

Lamb Fricassee

(Arnaki Fricassé)

Serves 6 • Preparation time 1 hour • Cooking time 1 hour and 30 minutes

INGREDIENTS

1 cup olive oil • 4 lbs lamb, cut into portions • salt and pepper • 2 lbs spring onions • 1 lb romaine lettuce • 1/2 cup finely chopped dill • 1/2 cup finely chopped parsley • 2 eggs • 1/2 cup lemon juice

In a heavy-bottomed stew pot sauté the meat portions in the oil, over high heat, until lightly browned all over. Pour in 1 cup hot water, add seasonings, and simmer, covered, for about 40 minutes, until the meat is half done. In the meantime, trim and wash the spring onions and the lettuce, chop coarsely, and drain. Add them along with the chopped dill and parsley to the casserole with the meat. Cover and cook gently, until the meat is tender and the vegetables are tender but firm. To prepare the egg-lemon sauce, lightly beat the eggs in a bowl, add the lemon juice, a little at a time, beating continuously. Gradually add a few tablespoons of the lamb broth, beating all the while. Then pour the mixture back in the pot. Shake the pot gently to distribute the sauce. Serve immediately.

Note: Spring onions may be parboiled and drained before being added to the meat. For a less caloric dish, substitute plain lemon juice for the egg-lemon sauce. Simply sprinkle it over the lamb and swirl the pot to mix it in.

Roast Lamb with Potatoes

(Arni sto Fourno me Patates)

Serves 6 • Preparation time 30 minutes • Cooking time 3 hours and 30 minutes

INGREDIENTS

1 leg of lamb (4 lbs) • 1/3 cup lemon juice • 1/3 cup olive oil • 4 lbs potatoes, peeled and quartered • 1/2 cup margarine or butter • salt, pepper, and oregano

Wash the meat and place it in a roasting pan. Rub it with lemon juice, reserving any left over, and sprinkle with salt and pepper. Add a little water to the pan and pour the oil over the meat. Preheat the oven to 300°F, cover the meat with aluminum foil, and roast for about 2 hours, basting now and then with the pan juices. Turn the meat over a few times to keep it moist. Add a little water when the juices boil down. Remove from the oven, surround the meat with the potatoes, season the potatoes with salt, pepper, and oregano, dot with the butter, and sprinkle with the reserved lemon juice. Raise the oven temperature to 350°F, return the pan to the oven, and roast for 1 hour and 30 minutes more, until the meat is tender and the potatoes are soft and lightly browned. Half an hour before serving time, take off the aluminum foil to brown the skin, or set the meat under the broiler for a few minutes. Let the meat rest for 5 or 10 minutes before carving.

Note: If desired, rub the leg of lamb with 3 cloves of crushed garlic, or cut the garlic into slivers and insert them into slits made all over the meat.

Pork with Leeks and Celery

(Hirino Prasoselino)

Serves 6 • Preparation time 30 minutes • Cooking time 1 hour and 30 minutes

INGREDIENTS

2 lbs celery root • 2 lbs leeks • 3/4 cup olive oil • 3 lbs pork shoulder, cut into serving portions • 1/2 cup grated onion • salt and freshly ground pepper • 2 eggs • 1/2 cup lemon juice

Wash and trim the celery root, clean and cut in quarters. Wash and trim the leeks. Cut in pieces. Blanch the celery and leeks in lightly salted boiling water, 8-10 minutes, and drain. Set aside. Heat the oil in a large cooking pan over high heat, and sauté the meat until lightly browned all over. Add the onions and, as they begin to brown, pour in 2 cups hot water. Add seasonings, cover, and simmer until the meat is tender and most of the water has evaporated. About 30 minutes before the meat is completely cooked, add the celery and leeks and continue to simmer until the celery is soft but firm. Do not overcook. To make the egg-lemon sauce, lightly beat the eggs in a bowl, then add the lemon juice, a little at a time, beating continuously. Gradually add a few tablespoons of the pan juices, beating all the while. Pour the mixture over the dish, shaking the pan gently to distribute the sauce. Allow the dish to stand 5 minutes before serving. Sprinkle with ground pepper and serve with feta cheese.

Note: Other meats may be substituted for the pork.

Meat-Stuffed Cabbage Rolls

(Dolmades me Lachano, Yiabrakia)

Serves 6-8 • Preparation time 1 hour • Cooking time 30-40 minutes

INGREDIENTS

1 large green cabbage • 1 lb ground beef • 1 lb ground pork • 1 cup grated onion • 1/2 cup short-grain rice • 1/2 cup finely chopped parsley • salt and pepper • 1/2 cup olive oil • 1/2 cup margarine or butter • Egg-Lemon Sauce or • Egg-Lemon Cream Sauce

Choose a cabbage with loose leaves. Wash well and, with a sharp, pointed knife, cut deeply around the core, and remove it to make the leaves separate more easily. Blanch the cabbage in lightly salted water for 10-15 minutes, until the outer leaves are soft and supple. Remove the cabbage, drain and, when cool enough to handle, carefully remove all the soft leaves, which should detach easily. Blanch the rest of the cabbage, until the remaining leaves are soft and separated. Trim the hard stems off the leaves and cut each into 2-3 pieces, large enough to roll. In a mixing bowl combine the meat, onion, rice, parsley, seasonings, and oil, and mix well. Line the bottom of a large shallow pan with 1-2 cabbage leaves that are torn. Place 1 tablespoon stuffing at the base of each leaf, fold the bottom over it, then fold in the sides, and roll the leaf up. Pack the rolls tightly into the pan, seam side down, in more than one layer, if necessary. Pour 1 cup boiling water over the rolls and dot with margarine or butter. Place a heavy plate upside down over the rolls to keep them in shape while cooking. Cover and simmer for 30-40 minutes, until the leaves are tender and the sauce reduced. Add more water if the dish seems dry. When ready, prepare the egg-lemon sauce, or egg-lemon cream sauce, and pour it over the rolls. For a less caloric dish, substitute plain

lemon juice for the egg-lemon sauce. Simply sprinkle it over the pan and shake to distribute evenly. Season with more freshly ground pepper and serve hot.

Meat-Stuffed Zucchini

(Kolokithakia me Kima)

Serves 6 • Preparation time 1 hour • Cooking time 1 hour and 30 minutes

INGREDIENTS

12 medium zucchini (about 4 lbs) • 1/2 cup olive oil • 1/2 cup grated onion • 1 lb ground beef • 1/2 cup short-grain rice • 1/2 cup finely chopped parsley • salt and freshly ground pepper • 1/2 cup melted margarine • 1-2 eggs • 1/2 cup lemon juice

Wash the zucchini and slice off both ends. Blanch them in lightly salted boiling water and drain. Using a potato peeler or a teaspoon, scoop out most of the flesh, leaving a thin layer next to the skin. Reserve the flesh for a zucchini pie. Gently heat the oil in a saucepan and sauté the onion, until transparent. Remove from the heat and mix with the ground meat, rice, parsley, salt, and pepper. Loosely fill the hollowed zucchini with the meat mixture, leaving room for expansion while cooking. Pack the stuffed zucchini closely into a heavy-bottomed, shallow pan and pour in 1½ cups hot water and the melted margarine. Cover and simmer for about 1 hour and 30 minutes, or until the meat is tender and the sauce reduced. Add a little more water if the dish seems dry. When ready, prepare an egg-lemon sauce and pour it over the dish, shaking the pan gently to distribute the sauce. For a lighter version, sprinkle the stuffed zucchini with plain lemon juice instead of the egg-lemon sauce. Season with freshly ground pepper and serve hot, accompanied by Greek Village Salad.

Meat-Stuffed Vine Leaves

(Dolmadakia me Kima)

Serves 6 • Preparation time 2 hours • Cooking time 40 minutes

INGREDIENTS

1 lb fresh or preserved vine leaves • 1 lb ground beef • 1 lb ground pork • 1 large onion, finely chopped • 1/2 cup finely chopped parsley • 1/2 cup finely chopped fresh dill or mint • 1/2 cup short-grain rice • 1 cup olive oil • 1/4 cup butter or margarine • 2 eggs • 1/3 cup lemon juice • salt and pepper

Wash the vine leaves and trim off the stems. Blanch them, a few at a time, in boiling water. Drain and cool. Mix the ground meat thoroughly with the onion, herbs, rice, seasonings, and half the oil. Line the bottom of a casserole with any torn or damaged vine leaves. Lay out a vine leaf flat (dull side up) and place about a tablespoon of the meat mixture in the middle of it. Fold over the sides, then roll up into a neat parcel. Repeat, until all the filling is used. Arrange the stuffed vine leaves in the pot, packing them in tightly, seam side down, to keep from unraveling while cooking. A second or more layers may be necessary. Pour in the remaining oil and 1 cup boiling water. Dot with the butter or margarine. Place a heavy plate upside down on top of the vine leaves to keep them in shape as they cook. Cover and simmer for 30-40 minutes or until the liquid is reduced by one third and the leaves are tender. Lightly beat the eggs in a bowl, add the lemon juice gradually, and continue beating. Very slowly pour 2-3 ladlefuls of hot liquid from the vine leaves into the egg mixture, beating all the time. Pour the egg-lemon sauce back over the stuffed vine leaves, shaking the pan gently to distribute it. Remove from the heat and sprinkle with freshly ground black pepper.

Alternate: The egg and lemon sauce, which is part of this recipe, can be replaced by a light savory white sauce.

Meat-Stuffed Eggplant

(Melitzanes Papoutsakia)

Serves 4-5 • Preparation time 2 hours • Baking time 1 hour

INGREDIENTS

4-5 small to medium eggplants (2½ lbs) • 1 lb ground lean meat (beef or veal) • 3 spring onions, finely chopped • 1 medium onion, grated • 1/2 cup finely chopped parsley • 2 cups chopped fresh or canned tomatoes • salt and freshly ground pepper • 1/2 cup olive oil • 1 egg • 3 tablespoons heavy cream • 1½ cups thick Béchamel • 2 egg yolks, lightly beaten • 1 cup grated kefalotiri or Romano cheese • 2 tomatoes, thinly sliced

Choose elongated eggplant. Wash, wipe dry, and cut off the stems. Halve the eggplant lengthwise, sprinkle liberally with salt and place in a colander for 1-2 hours. Rinse with cold water and squeeze out the excess water with your hands. In a large frying pan, fry the eggplant in olive oil over medium heat, until they are golden brown. Arrange them closely in an oiled ovenproof dish, flesh side up, and set aside. Sauté the onion in the oil, until transparent, mix in the ground meat, and sauté until lightly colored, approximately 10 minutes. Add the tomatoes, parsley, seasonings, and toss briefly over high heat. Then reduce the heat and simmer, covered, until the sauce is very thick. Remove from the heat and allow the mixture to cool slightly. Beat the egg and cream lightly, and mix into the meat mixture. With the back of a large spoon, press down the flesh of the eggplant halves, making space for the stuffing. Put 2-3 tablespoons of meat mixture in each half eggplant and spread evenly. Prepare the béchamel and fold in the egg yolks and half the grated cheese. Spoon a small amount of béchamel sauce over the meat, smooth the surface, and place a tomato slice on top. Sprinkle with the remaining grated cheese and a dash of pepper. Pour a little water into the baking dish, preheat the oven to 350°F, and bake for about 1 hour, until the tops are golden brown. Serve hot.

Veal Stew with Eggplant

(Moschari Kokkinisto me Melitzanes)

Serves 5-6 • Preparation time 2 hours • Cooking time 1 hour and 30 minutes

INGREDIENTS

Veal Stew recipe (page 59) • 4 lbs eggplant • olive oil and vegetable oil for frying • 2 small tomatoes, thinly sliced • 1 green bell pepper, cut in small squares

Prepare the complete recipe for Meat Stew. In the meantime, wash, trim, and cut the eggplant in round or lengthwise slices, according to your preference. Sprinkle them generously with salt and allow to stand for about 2 hours in a colander. Then rinse them under the tap, squeeze out the water with your hands, and fry them in hot oil until light brown. Place the fried eggplant in the pot with the meat, fold in carefully, and simmer, covered, over low heat, for about 10 minutes. For a more festive presentation, lay two long fried eggplant slices one on top of the other to form a cross, place one cube of the cooked meat in the center, and fold the ends of the eggplant slices over the meat, to make a parcel. Put a slice of tomato, and a piece of green pepper on top and secure them with a wooden toothpick. Repeat the

process until all the meat cubes or the eggplant slices are used. Arrange the parcels closely in a shallow glass baking dish and pour the sauce over them. Sprinkle with a little seasoning. Preheat oven to 400°F and bake for 15-20 minutes. Serve hot.

Poultry and Game

(Poulerika ke Kinigi)

Chicken with Peppers and Onions

(Kotopoulo me Piperies ke Kremmidia)

Serves 4-5 • Preparation time 30 minutes • Cooking time 1 hour

INGREDIENTS

1 cup olive oil • 2 lbs onions, thinly sliced • 1½ lbs long green peppers, cut into rings • 2 garlic cloves, sliced (optional) • 1 large chicken, cut into serving pieces • 1 cup chopped fresh or canned tomatoes • 1/2 cup red wine or • 2 tablespoons vinegar • 1 tablespoon tomato paste • 2 tablespoons minced parsley or 1 bay leaf • salt and pepper • 2 tablespoons heavy cream (optional)

Heat the oil in a heavy-bottomed frying pan and sauté the onions and garlic, followed by the peppers. Remove with a perforated spoon to a bowl. In the same pan lightly brown the chicken pieces on all sides. Return the sautéed vegetables to the frying pan, add the tomatoes, wine, tomato paste, parsley, and season to taste. Stir gently, cover, and cook slowly, until the chicken and vegetables are tender and the juices are reduced. Add the cream, stir, and remove from the heat. Serve the dish with pilaf or steamed potatoes.

Roast Lemon Chicken

(Kotopoulo Lemonato Fournou)

Serves 4-5 • Preparation time 30 minutes • Baking time 1 hour and 30 minutes

INGREDIENTS

1 large chicken • 1/2 cup lemon juice • salt, pepper, and oregano • 1/2 cup olive oil • 4 lbs potatoes, peeled and sliced • 1/2 cup butter, cubed

Wash the chicken and drain well. Rub the chicken inside and out with half the lemon juice, salt, pepper, and oregano. Place the chicken, breast side up, in a roasting pan. Coat with oil and surround with potatoes. Pour the remaining lemon juice over the potatoes, season them with salt, pepper, and oregano, and dot with the butter cubes. Cover with aluminum foil, preheat the oven to 350°F, and bake for about 1 hour and 30 minutes, or until the chicken and potatoes are soft and most of the juices have been absorbed. Add a little hot water if the dish seems dry. Half an hour before the dish is completely cooked, remove the foil to brown, or place under the broiler for a few minutes before serving.

Stuffed Turkey

(Galopoula Yemisti)

Serves about 10 • Preparation time, about 1 hour and 30 minutes • Cooking time depends on the weight of bird

INGREDIENTS

1 turkey (8-10 lbs) • 1/4 cup lemon juice • 1/2 cup orange juice • 1/2 cup butter • salt and pepper
THE STUFFING: 1/3 cup butter • turkey giblets (liver, heart, gizzard) • 1/2 lb ground beef • 1/2 lb ground pork or lamb • 1 small onion, finely chopped • 1/4 cup short-grain rice • 1/2 lb chestnuts, boiled, shelled, and chopped • 1/4 cup pine nuts • 1/4 cup currants (optional) • 2 tablespoons brandy (optional) • 2 cups Chicken or Meat Stock
THE GARNISH: 1 lb chestnuts, boiled and shelled • 1 lb dried prunes, pitted • 1 lb dried apricots • 3 large quinces or cooking apples • 4 cups Meat Stock • 1 cup butter • salt and pepper

Remove the innards. Wash the turkey and pat dry. Melt the butter, blend with the lemon and orange juices, and rub the turkey with the mixture inside and out. Reserve the remaining liquid. Sprinkle the turkey cavities and skin with salt and pepper. Set aside.

Prepare the stuffing: Wash the giblets and chop them. Heat the butter in a saucepan, and sauté the onion until transparent. Add the chopped giblets and ground meat. Brown them lightly. Add half the meat stock and all the other stuffing ingredients and mix well. Remove from the heat, adjust the seasonings, and allow to cool. You may cook the stuffing separately, if you wish, as follows. After the chopped giblets and ground meat are browned, add the beef stock, cover, and simmer for 10 minutes. Add the rice and continue simmering, for about 20 minutes, until the rice is soft. Add the remaining ingredients and stir well. Remove from the heat, place a thick piece of paper towel or a cotton dish cloth between the lid and the pan, and let rest for 5 minutes before serving.

To stuff the turkey: Place the turkey, breast side down, on a cutting board. Spoon in enough of the uncooked stuffing to loosely fill the neck cavity. Fold the neck skin over the back, close the neck opening, and truss with a piece of string. Fold the wing tips back and under the bird's backbone. Turn the turkey over, breast side up, on the board. Fill the body cavity with the rest of the stuffing and sew up the vent with a trussing needle. Do not overfill the bird as the stuffing will expand while cooking. With a long piece of string tie and secure the legs to the tail. Place the turkey, breast side up, in a large, shallow pan. Add water to cover the bottom of the pan. Cover the breast and drumsticks with aluminum foil leaving the sides open. Preheat oven to 325°F and roast for half an hour per pound. Add water frequently during roasting. Baste the turkey with the reserved butter and juices mixture from time to time. When the bird is almost cooked, remove the foil to brown. Transfer the turkey to a platter. Pour the remaining stock into the roasting pan, mix with the pan juices, and stir well to scrape up any bits of meat stuck to the bottom. Pour the mixture into a saucepan, skim off most of the fat, and reduce the sauce over medium heat.

To prepare the garnish: Cook the chestnuts, prunes, and apricots separately, each in 1 cup meat stock, with 1/4 cup butter. Boil until all the liquid evaporates and the fruits are glazed with the butter. Wash and rub the quince until the skin shines. Cut into eighths and remove the seeds. Boil the quince in 1 cup meat stock with 1/3 cup butter, and seasonings until all the liquid evaporates. Season to taste with 2 tablespoons sugar, a little nutmeg, allspice, and freshly ground black pepper. Shake the pan gently, to distribute the seasonings. Place the turkey on a large platter, and surround with the buttered chestnuts, prunes, apricots, and quince. Serve the gravy separately.

Hare and Onion Stew

(Lagos Stifado)

Serves 6 • Preparation time 24-48 hours • Cooking time 2 hours

INGREDIENTS

4 lbs hare, cut into portions • 1 cup olive oil • 4 lbs stewing or pearl onions • salt and pepper • 3 cups puréed fresh or canned tomatoes

THE MARINADE: 1/2 cup olive oil • 1 cup dry red wine • 2 tablespoons vinegar • 3 bay leaves • 20 peppercorns • 10 allspice berries • 4 garlic cloves

Wash hare pieces with water and vinegar. Prepare the marinade, add the hare, cover, and refrigerate for 2-4 days. Turn and baste the meat 4-6 times. Remove the meat from the marinade and strain the sauce in a bowl, reserving the spices. Cut off the tops and tails of the onions, blanch for about 1 minute, drain, and peel. Heat the oil in a large heavy-bottomed pot, and sauté the onions in batches until lightly browned. Remove each batch with a slotted spoon. In the same pot, brown the meat lightly all over. Pour in the reserved marinade and season to taste. From the reserved spices, add 2 bay leaves, 6 peppercorns, and 6 allspice. Add the tomatoes, cover, and bring to a boil. Then reduce the heat and simmer for about 30 minutes. Add the sautéed onions and 3 of the reserved garlic cloves. Cover and continue simmering, for about 90 minutes, or until the meat and onions are tender and the sauce is very thick. If, when the onions and meat are ready, the sauce has not reduced to the required consistency, strain and boil it down rapidly. Pour it back over the stew. Serve hot with Boiled Beets.

Rabbit or other game or poultry is also excellent prepared this way.

Veal or Beef Stew

(Moschari Kokkinisto)

Serves 5-6 • Preparation time 30 minutes • Cooking time 1 hour and 30 minutes

INGREDIENTS

1/2 cup olive oil • 3 lbs veal, lamb, or beef tenderloin, cut into portions • 1 medium onion, finely chopped • 3 cups puréed fresh or canned tomatoes • 1/4 cup finely chopped parsley (optional) • 1 tablespoon vinegar (optional) • 1 teaspoon sugar • salt and pepper

Heat the oil in a heavy-bottomed pan. Add the meat, a few pieces at a time, and sauté until lightly browned all over. Add the onion and sauté 2-3 minutes until transparent. Add the tomatoes, parsley, vinegar, sugar, salt, and pepper. Stir and simmer, covered, for about 90 minutes, or until the meat is tender and the sauce is thick. Add a small amount of hot water if the dish seems too dry. Serve accompanied by french fried potatoes, pasta, or rice and a green salad.

Wild Boar with Cabbage

(Agriogourouno me Lachano)

Serves 6 • Preparation time 30 minutes • Cooking time 1 hour and 30 minutes

INGREDIENTS

4 lbs cabbage • 2 cups olive oil • 3 lbs wild boar shoulder, cut in portions • 1/2 cup grated onion (optional) • 2 cups tomato purée • salt and freshly ground pepper • 2-3 tablespoons vinegar

Discard the outer leaves of the cabbage and trim off the core. Cut the cabbage into pieces and wash. Parboil for 5 minutes in lightly salted water, drain, and set aside. In a heavy-bottomed saucepan, sauté the meat in oil over high heat, until lightly browned all over. Add the onion and sauté lightly. Pour in the tomato. Add the seasonings and simmer, covered, until the meat is almost tender. Add the cabbage and vinegar, and continue simmering until the cabbage is soft and the sauce is reduced. Add a little water if the dish seems dry. Serve hot. **Note:** Other meats can be substituted for the wild boar.

Fish and Seafood

(Psaria ke Thalassina)

Skewered Swordfish

(Xifias Souvlaki)

Serves 4 • Preparation time 1 hour • Grilling time 15-20 minutes

INGREDIENTS

2 lbs swordfish • 1 large onion • 1 large green bell pepper • 1 large tomato • 1 chili pepper (optional) • salt and pepper • 12 small skewers

Wash and drain the fish well, cut into 1½ inch cubes. Cut the onion, green pepper, and tomato into cubes about the same size. Thread the fish onto skewers, alternating with onion, pepper, and tomato cubes. If using chili pepper, add a small piece to each skewer, or more if desired. Brush with oil, sprinkle with seasonings, and grill over charcoal or under the broiler. Baste with oil and turn twice. Cook for about 15 minutes, or until the fish is done to your taste. Do not overcook. Spread with Oil-Lemon Dressing and serve immediately.

Grilled Porgies or Sea Bream

(Tsipoures sti Skara)

Serves 4 • Preparation time 15 minutes • Grilling time 20 minutes

INGREDIENTS

4 porgies or other sea bream (about 1 lb each) • salt and pepper • olive oil • Oil-Lemon Dressing • finely chopped parsley

Have your fish dealer scale and clean the fish. Wash and drain them well. Make 2-3 shallow, diagonal incisions on both sides of each fish. Rub with a little salt and pepper, and brush the fish with oil inside and out. Place on a preheated grill rack (preheating the rack will prevent the fish from sticking). Grill the fish over charcoal or under the broiler for 10-15 minutes on each side, basting occasionally with oil. Place on a platter, moisten the fish with oil-lemon dressing, and sprinkle with chopped parsley. Serve immediately, accompanied by Boiled Greens or Tomato and Onion Salad.

Sea bream Spetses-Style

(Sinagrida Spetsiotiki)

Serves 5-6 • Preparation time 1 hour and 30 minutes • Cooking time 1 hour

INGREDIENTS

1 whole sea bream, porgy, red snapper (about 3 lbs) or • 5-6 slices of any large fish • 1/4 cup lemon juice • 1 cup olive oil • salt, pepper, and flour • 1 large onion, thinly sliced • 4 garlic cloves, chopped • 1½ lbs fresh tomatoes, chopped • 1/2 cup dry white wine • 1/2 cup finely chopped parsley

Have your fish dealer clean and scale the fish. Rinse and drain, patting dry with paper towels. With a sharp knife, score the fish along the backbone on both sides. Place in a baking pan, rub the fish with lemon juice and seasonings, and sprinkled with a little flour. Pour half the oil over the fish and let it stand for 1 hour. Heat the remaining oil in a saucepan and sauté the onion and garlic until transparent. Add the tomatoes, wine, and parsley, and simmer, covered, until the sauce is very thick. Preheat the oven to 325°F, pour the sauce over the fish, and bake for about 1 hour. Baste the fish occasionally with the pan juices.

Fried Salted Cod

(Bakaliaros Pastos Tiganitos)

Serves 4 • Preparation time 18-20 hours • Frying time 15-20 minutes

INGREDIENTS

2 lbs salted cod • oil for frying

THE BATTER: 3 eggs • salt and pepper • self-raising flour

THE GARNISH: parsley sprigs, lemon slices

Remove the skin and cut the fish into 3-inch serving or bite-size pieces. Rinse off loose salt under the tap. Soak in cold water, refrigerated, for 18-20 hours, changing the water several times, until the fish is only lightly salted. Remove the bones and drain the fish thoroughly. **Prepare the batter:** In a bowl lightly beat the eggs with 3-4 tablespoons water until fluffy. Stir in enough flour to make a medium thick batter. Adjust the seasonings and set aside. In a large skillet, pour oil to a depth of 1/2 inch. Heat until the oil reaches the smoking point. Dip the cod pieces one by one into the batter and drop into the hot oil. Lower heat to medium and fry until lightly browned on both sides (approximately 4 minutes per side). Fry only a few pieces at a time. Remove with a slotted spoon and drain on paper towels. Arrange on a platter, garnished with parsley sprigs and lemon slices. Serve hot with garlic sauce and Boiled Greens.

Baked Small Fish

(Gavros Plaki)

Serves 4 • Preparation time 1 hour • Baking time 1 hour

INGREDIENTS

3 lbs small fish (picarel, anchovies, sardines) • 1 cup olive oil • 4 large onions, sliced • 6 garlic cloves, sliced • 2 tablespoons tomato paste • 1/4 cup white wine or fish stock or water • 1 cup finely chopped parsley • salt and pepper to taste • 2 fresh tomatoes, sliced • 3 thin lemon slices, peeled

Clean the fish, removing heads and back bones, if desired. Wash and drain well. Heat the oil in a saucepan, add the onions and garlic, and sauté until transparent. Dilute the tomato paste in the wine and pour it over the onions. Add parsley and season to taste. Cover and simmer, until all the liquid has evaporated. In a "yiouvetsi" (clay) or other ovenproof dish, place half the fish combined with half the tomato and lemon slices. Cover with half the sauce, add the remaining fish, tomatoes, and lemon slices, and spread the remaining sauce on top. Preheat oven to 400°F and bake for 30-40 minutes. Equally good hot or cold.

Squid with Onions

(Kalamaria Stifado)

Serves 4 • Preparation time 30 minutes • Cooking time 1 hour and 30 minutes

INGREDIENTS

2 lbs squid • 1 cup olive oil • 2 lbs onions, thinly sliced or pearl onions • 6 garlic cloves • 3 tablespoons tomato paste • 1 cup white wine • 2 bay leaves • 3 allspice berries • 10 peppercorns • salt and pepper • 1/2 teaspoon sugar

Wash the squid thoroughly in cold water. Detach the head from the body. Using a sharp knife, sever the tentacles from the rest of the head, cutting just above the eyes (do not sever the tentacles). Squeeze out the beak and discard. Discard the rest of head with viscera and ink sac. Slip out the cartilage strip and discard. Wash under running water and peel off the translucent membrane. Rinse well inside and out. If the squid are very small, leave whole. If large, cut into rings. Place in a colander, drain, and pat dry with paper towels. Heat the oil in a large heavy-bottomed pan, add the onions and garlic, and sauté until transparent. Add the squid and sauté until all the liquid has evaporated. Dilute the tomato paste in the wine and pour it over the squid. Add the rest of the ingredients and stir. Cover and simmer over medium heat, until the squid are tender and the sauce is thick. Alternate: Cuttlefish or octopus may be used instead of squid. For cuttlefish, follow the squid recipe. For octopus, prepare according to the recipe for Octopus in Vinegar (page 14). After you peel off the skin, cut it in small pieces and follow the squid recipe. Add more water if the dish seems dry and simmer until the octopus is tender and the sauce has thickened.

Cuttlefish with Spinach

(Soupies me Spanaki)

Serves 4 • Preparation time 1 hour • Cooking time 40 minutes

INGREDIENTS

2 lbs cuttlefish (fresh or frozen) • 3/4 cup olive oil • 1 large onion, sliced • 1 tablespoon tomato paste • 1/2 cup white wine • salt and pepper • 2 lbs fresh or frozen spinach • 1/2 cup finely chopped dill • freshly ground pepper

Clean the cuttlefish, discarding inc sac, viscera, outer membrane, and cuttlebone. Cut in pieces, wash, drain, and pat dry with paper towels. Heat the oil in a large pot, add the onion, and sauté until transparent. Add the cuttlefish and sauté until all the liquid has evaporated. Dilute the tomato paste in the wine and pour it over the cuttlefish. Stir in the seasonings. Cover and simmer for about 10 minutes until the cuttlefish are almost tender. Add a little hot water, if necessary. If using fresh spinach, blanch for 5 minutes in boiling water and drain. Frozen spinach should be added directly to the pot. Add the spinach and dill to the cuttlefish, stir, cover, and simmer for about 20 minutes until the spinach is done and the sauce is thick. Sprinkle with freshly ground pepper and serve. Equally good cold.

Sweets

(Glika)

Ravani

(Ravani)

Serves 20 • Preparation time 45 minutes • Baking time 35 minutes

INGREDIENTS

1 ⅓ cups fine semolina • 1 ⅓ cups self-raising flour • 1½ teaspoons baking powder • 8 eggs • 1 ⅓ cups sugar • 1/4 cup lukewarm milk • 2 teaspoons vanilla

THE SYRUP: 3 cups sugar • 2½ cups water • 6 tablespoons butter • 2 tablespoons lemon juice • 1½ teaspoons grated lemon rind • 20 blanched almond halves for garnish

Mix together semolina, flour, and baking powder in a bowl. Beat the eggs and sugar with an electric mixer at high speed for about 15 minutes, until thick and fluffy. Beating continuously, add the milk, a tablespoon at a time; then add the flavoring. Stop beating. Gently fold in the mixed dry ingredients, taking care not to break down the air bubbles beaten into the eggs. The batter should be light and foamy. Pour the mixture, spreading it evenly into a well-greased, round baking pan 12 inches in diameter. Preheat the oven to 350°F and bake for 30-35 minutes. The cake is ready when the edges begin to shrink from the sides of the pan. Meanwhile, prepare the syrup. Dissolve the sugar in the water over medium heat; then boil for 5 minutes. Add the lemon juice, butter, and lemon rind. Remove from the heat, and ladle it over the lukewarm cake, slowly and evenly. When completely cold, cut the ravani into wedges, arrange them on a serving dish, and place one halved almond on each. Keep refrigerated.

Baked Quinces

(Kidonia Psita)

Serves 8 • Preparation time 20 minutes • Baking time 1 hour and 30 minutes

INGREDIENTS

4 large quinces • 1½ cups sugar • 2 tablespoons lemon juice • whole cloves (optional)

Wash the quinces thoroughly and rub them dry with a cloth to remove the fuzz and polish the skin. Cut the fruit into 4-6 wedges, depending on the size, and remove the cores. Arrange the quince wedges, cut side up, in a buttered, ovenproof dish or pan. Sprinkle them with the sugar. Put the cores in a saucepan with 1 cup of water. Cover and simmer for about 10 minutes. Strain the juice, mix in the lemon juice, and sprinkle the liquid over the quinces. Cover with aluminum foil, preheat the oven to 350°F and bake slowly for 30 minutes. Remove the foil, turn the quinces upside down in the pan, and stick a clove into each one. Bake them, uncovered, until they are soft and golden. Let them cool slightly in the pan. The cooking liquid will gel as it cools. Transfer the quinces to a serving dish and pour one tablespoonful of the warm jelly over each one. Serve the baked quinces warm or cold, topped with whipped cream, a scoop of ice cream, or a dollop of strained yogurt.

Baklava

(Baklavas)

Yields 30 pieces • Preparation time 1 hour and 15 minutes • Baking time 1 hour

INGREDIENTS

2 cups chopped almonds • 2 cups chopped walnuts • 2 teaspoons cinnamon • 1/2 teaspoon ground cloves • 1½ cups unsalted butter, clarified • 1 lb packaged phyllo or • 1 recipe, Homemade Phyllo Pastry • whole cloves for garnish • THE SYRUP: 3 cups sugar • 2 cups water • 1/2 cup glucose or honey • 1 teaspoon vanilla or • the grated rind of one lemon, or • 2 tablespoons brandy

Mix the first 4 ingredients in a bowl. Set aside. Use a baking sheet the size of the phyllo pastry. If it is smaller, cut the entire stack of phyllo sheets into rectangles or rounds to just fit in pan. Melt the butter. (Brush any pastry trimmings with melted butter, and scatter them between the layers as you assemble the baklava.) Generously grease the baking pan with butter. Place 4 buttered phyllo sheets over the bottom, one on top of the other and sprinkle some of the nut mixture evenly over them. The multiple layer effect of a baklava is achieved by spreading the nut filling on every second phyllo sheet. Layer the phyllo sheets, buttering between each layer and sprinkle the nut mixture over every second layer until there is no filling left. Cover the top with 4 buttered phyllo sheets. Score the top layers with a sharp-pointed knife into small diamond-shaped pieces. Stick a clove in the center of each. Brush with the remaining melted butter and sprinkle the surface with a little warm water to prevent the phyllo from curling up. Preheat the oven to 350°F and bake for 1 hour or until golden brown. Meanwhile, prepare the syrup. Boil all the ingredients in a heavy-bottomed pan, for 5 minutes. For extra flavor add vanilla, lemon rind, or brandy to the syrup. If using lemon rind, boil it with the syrup ingredients. Vanilla or brandy should be added after removing the syrup from the heat. Ladle the hot syrup over the baklava as soon as you remove it from the oven. Let it absorb the syrup and cool completely. Baklava will keep at room temperature from one to two weeks.

Kataifi

(Kataifi)

Yields 30-35 pieces • Preparation time 1 hour • Baking time 1 hour

INGREDIENTS

1 lb chopped walnuts • 1/4 cup rusk crumbs • 2 tablespoons cinnamon • 1 teaspoon grated lemon rind or • 1 teaspoon ground cloves • 3 tablespoons brandy • 1 lb kataifi pastry • 2 cups unsalted butter clarified • THE SYRUP: 6 cups sugar • 4 cups water • 1/2 cup glucose • 1-2 sticks of cinnamon or • 1 teaspoon grated lemon rind • chopped pistachio nuts for topping

Mix the first 6 ingredients into a bowl and sprinkle with the brandy. Fluff up the kataifi pastry and divide into 30-35 portions. Keep covered with a damp cloth, as the pastry dries quickly. Take one portion and spread it to form a long strip. Put 1-2 tablespoons of nut mixture at one end and roll it up. It is important to roll the pastry loosely because it contracts as it bakes. Continue the same procedure with the rest of pastry portions. Pack the rolls in a greased baking pan just large enough to

hold them. Melt the butter and dribble it slowly and evenly over the rolls. (At this stage you may freeze the kataifi rolls. Allow them to thaw out before baking.) Preheat the oven to 300°F, and bake for 1 hour and 30 minutes or until tops and sides are crisp and golden brown. Meanwhile, prepare the syrup. Heat all the syrup ingredients in a heavy-bottomed pan and boil for 5 minutes. Remove the rolls from the oven. Ladle a little syrup over each roll and as it is absorbed, pour over the remaining syrup. Allow the kataifi rolls to cool completely before you transfer them to a serving dish. Sprinkle the tops with chopped pistachios. Keep the rolls uncovered so they will stay crisp. They keep well at room temperature from one to two weeks.

Almond Christmas Cookies

(Kourabiedes)

Yields 50-60 pieces • Preparation time 20 minutes • Baking time 20 minutes

INGREDIENTS

1 cup unsalted butter, clarified • 1 cup shortening • 1/2 cup confectioners' sugar • 3 teaspoons vanilla • 4-5 cups all-purpose flour • 1 cup blanched almonds, roasted and coarsely chopped • rose water (optional) • confectioners' sugar for dusting

Cream the butter, shortening, and sugar with the mixer until light and fluffy. Add the flavoring and stop beating. Fold in the flour a little at a time, blending lightly by hand. Then fold in the almonds, and knead lightly, adding more flour until the dough is light and does not stick to the fingers. Avoid overworking the dough. Too much handling will make them stiff. Roll the dough into crescent shapes, or cut it with a star-shaped cookie cutter, and place on a baking sheet. Preheat the oven to 350°F and bake for about 20 minutes, or until lightly golden. Remove from the oven and immediately transfer with a spatula to greaseproof paper, liberally dusted with confectioners' sugar. Sprinkle with rose water, and sift lots of confectioners' sugar over them. Let the Kourabiedes cool before you transfer them to a serving dish. Stored in a cookie tin, they keep well up to one month.

Honey-Dipped Cookies

(Melomakarona)

Yields 40-50 cookies • Preparation time 30 minutes • Baking time 30 minutes

INGREDIENTS

8 cups all-purpose flour • 1 teaspoon baking soda • 2 teaspoons baking powder • 1½ cups olive oil • 1/2 cup shortening • 1 cup sugar • 3/4 cup orange juice • 1/4 cup brandy • 2 teaspoons grated orange rind • THE SYRUP: 2 cups honey • 2 cups sugar • 2 cups water

THE GARNISH: 1½ cups finely chopped walnuts • 1 teaspoon cinnamon • 1/2 teaspoon ground cloves

Sift together the flour, soda, and baking powder into a kneading basin, and make a well in the center. Blend the remaining ingredients at high speed in a food processor or blender. Pour the mixture into the well. Gradually incorporate the flour from the sides of the well into the liquid and knead lightly until you have a soft, greasy dough. Do not overknead. Roll out the dough into a sheet 1/3-inch thick. Use cookie cutters to cut the dough into ovals, squares, or rounds. Arrange them on ungreased baking sheets and decorate the tops by drawing and pressing the prongs of a fork across the surface. Preheat the oven to 350°F and bake for about 30 minutes or until golden brown. Meanwhile, combine the syrup ingredients in a large pan and bring them to a boil. Lower the heat and simmer for 7 minutes. Skim off the froth and pour the syrup over the cookies as soon as they come out of the oven. When all the syrup is absorbed, turn them over and allow to cool completely. Mix together the walnuts, cinnamon, and cloves. Turn over one cookie at a time, and sprinkle the tops with the walnut mixture. Place the cookies on a platter and keep covered with plastic wrap to prevent from drying out. They keep well at room temperature up to 3 weeks.

Fried Pastry Coils

(Diples)

Yields 60 diples • Preparation time 1 hour • Frying time 1 hour

INGREDIENTS

THE DOUGH: 2 eggs and 4 egg yolks • 6 tablespoons orange juice • 1 tablespoon sugar • 2 tablespoons olive oil • 4 cups all-purpose flour • 2 tablespoons finely grated orange rind

THE SYRUP: 1/2 cup honey • 1 cup sugar • 1/2 cup water

THE GARNISH: 2 cups finely chopped walnuts • 2 teaspoons cinnamon • oil for frying

Lightly beat the eggs and egg yolks in a mixing bowl. Stir in the orange juice, sugar, oil, and grated orange rind. Gradually add enough flour, kneading well, until you have a rather soft, elastic dough. Divide the dough into 8 equal portions and roll them into balls. Cover the balls with plastic wrap and let them stand for 1 hour. On a floured surface, roll out each ball into a sheet as thin as possible. Sprinkle the surface frequently with cornstarch to prevent sticking. Cut the pastry sheets into strips 12 inches long and 2 inches wide. Heat the oil in a deep fryer until it registers 375°F. Place one edge of each strip between the prongs of a fork and secure it by wrapping it around the fork twice. Hold the other edge of the strip with your other hand. Dip the fork with the dough into the boiling oil, twirl the fork around, and wrap the remaining ribbon of dough slowly around the fork as it fries. Fry until golden; it should not brown. Remove with a slotted spoon and place on absorbent paper to drain. Repeat with the rest of the dough. Put the syrup ingredients in a saucepan. Bring to a boil and skim off the froth. Drop in the diples, a few at a time, let them stand for 1-2 minutes, and transfer to a serving dish. Mix the walnuts and cinnamon, and sprinkle over diples . as soon as you remove them from the honey. They keep well for several weeks at room temperature.

Alternative: If this procedure seems too complicated, simply cut the dough into squares or rectangles and fry them on both sides. They will not be as pretty but they will taste just as good.

Honey Puffs

(Loukoumades)

Yields 100 puffs • Preparation time 1 hour • Frying time 1 hour

INGREDIENTS

THE DOUGH: 2 oz fresh yeast or • 2 tablespoons dry yeast • 3½ cups all-purpose flour • 1 cup tepid water • 1 cup tepid milk • 1 tablespoon sugar • 1 teaspoon salt • 4 tablespoons oil • oil for frying

THE GARNISH: Honey, cinnamon, finely chopped walnuts

Dissolve the yeast in the tepid water. Combine it with the remaining dough ingredients in the bowl of an electric mixer. Beat at high speed until you have a smooth batter. Cover and let it rise in a warm place until it triples in size, 1-2 hours. To speed up the procedure, place the dough in a warm oven (90°F). When ready to serve, heat the oil in a large pan to 375°F. Moisten one of your hands and take a handful of the dough. Clench your fist and gently squeeze out a small ball of dough the size of a walnut. Cut off the dough with a wet spoon, and drop it into the

hot oil. Dip the spoon in water every time you cut the dough to prevent sticking. Fry the loukoumades a few at a time, pushing them into the oil with a slotted spoon, until they turn a crisp golden-brown. Remove with the slotted spoon, drain on paper towels, and transfer to a serving dish. Pour hot honey over them and dust lightly with cinnamon. Sprinkle with chopped walnuts. Serve immediately. If the honey is too thick, boil it with a little water. Skim off the froth before using.

Custard Pastry

(Galaktoboureko)

Serves 14 • Preparation time 30 minutes • Baking time 50 minutes

INGREDIENTS

4 cups milk • 3 eggs and 2 egg yolks • 1/2 cup sugar • 1/3 cup and 1 tablespoon fine semolina • 2 teaspoons vanilla • 1/2 lb phyllo pastry • 1/2 cup hot, melted, clarified, unsalted butter

THE SYRUP: 1½ cups sugar • 1 cup water • 1 tablespoon lemon juice • 1 teaspoon vanilla

Boil the milk and cool slightly. Beat the eggs and sugar with an electric mixer, until light and creamy. Add the semolina and mix well with a wooden spoon. Transfer the mixture into a large heavy-bottomed saucepan. Stirring constantly, pour in the hot milk. Cook the mixture, stirring over low heat, until you have a smooth textured cream, about 10 minutes. Remove from the heat, stir in the flavoring and 3-4 tablespoons of the butter. Grease an 8 by 12 inch cake pan. Cut the phyllo sheets into rectangles the size of the pan. Spread half the phyllo sheets over the bottom of the pan, brushing each one with melted butter. Brush any pastry trimmings with melted butter, too, and scatter them between the layers. Pour in the cream and spread it evenly over the pastry. Brush each of the remaining sheets with melted butter and lay them on top of each other on a flat surface. Cut them lengthwise into 4 strips, without cutting through the edges so that each sheet stays intact. Lift the strips of phyllo carefully and place them lightly on top of the custard. Brush the surface with butter and sprinkle a little warm water to prevent the phyllo from curling up while baking. Preheat the oven to 375°F and bake for about 15 minutes, then lower the temperature to 325°F and bake for another 35 minutes or until the top is golden brown. To make the syrup, put the ingredients in a saucepan and bring to a boil. Let boil for 7 minutes. Ladle the syrup slowly over the pastry as soon as you remove it from the oven. Allow it to absorb the syrup and cool slightly before eating. Cut the Galaktoboureko into pieces and serve warm or cold, preferably on the day it is made. Keep any leftovers in the refrigerator, uncovered so they remain crisp.

Custard Pie

(Bougatsa me Krema)

Serves 8-10 • Preparation time 30 minutes • Baking time 30 minutes

INGREDIENTS

4 cups milk • 1/2 cup butter • 2/3 cup fine semolina • 2/3 cup sugar • 2 whole eggs and 2 egg yolks • 1 teaspoon vanilla • 1 lb packaged phyllo • 2/3 cup melted butter • confectioners' sugar • cinnamon

Heat the milk to boiling. In another saucepan heat the butter, pour in the semolina, and sauté for 1-2 minutes. Off the heat, pour in the hot milk all at once, stirring constantly. Return to the heat. Add the sugar. Simmer, stirring, until creamy and thick, the consistency of custard. Remove from the heat. While the custard is cooling for 5 minutes, lightly beat the eggs and egg yolks. Pour the eggs and the vanilla into the custard, stirring constantly until smooth. Set aside. (To prevent a skin forming, place a sheet of plastic wrap over the surface of the cream.) On a lightly buttered baking sheet, the size of the phyllo, lay down a sheet of phyllo, brush with the melted butter, and add another sheet. Repeat until half the phyllo sheets, approximately 10 of them, have been used. (A 1-pound packet of phyllo usually contains 20 sheets.) Pour the custard mixture over them and spread evenly. Cover with the rest of the phyllo, brushing each sheet with melted butter. Preheat oven to 400°F and bake until the phyllo is golden brown. Cut into squares and serve hot, sprinkled with confectioners' sugar and powdered cinnamon.

Walnut Cake with Syrup
(Karidopita)

Serves 16 • Preparation time 30 minutes • Baking time 35 minutes

INGREDIENTS

6 eggs • 1 cup sugar • 1 cup rusk crumbs • 1½ teaspoons baking powder • 2 teaspoons cinnamon • 1/4 teaspoon ground cloves • 1½ cups finely chopped walnuts

THE SYRUP: 2 cups sugar • 2 cups water • 2 tablespoons corn syrup or • 1 tablespoon lemon juice • 3 tablespoons brandy • confectioners' sugar for dusting

Beat the eggs and sugar with an electric mixer at high speed until they triple in bulk and fall from the whisk in a thick ribbon, about 15 minutes. Meanwhile, mix together the crumbs, baking powder, spices, and nuts. Gently fold the nut mixture into the beaten eggs, sprinkling it on lightly as you fold. Light handling is very important at this stage because the air beaten into the eggs keeps the cake light. Pour the mixture into a well greased and floured, round cake pan 10 inches in diameter and smooth the surface. Preheat the oven to 350°F and bake for 30-35 minutes. The cake is done when the edges begin to shrink from the sides of the pan and the top feels springy to the touch. Meanwhile, prepare the syrup. Dissolve the sugar in the water over medium heat, add the lemon juice, and boil the syrup for 5 minutes. Cool slightly and stir in the brandy. Ladle the syrup over the cooled cake, slowly and evenly. Allow the cake to cool completely before you cut and serve.

Semolina Halva
(Halvas Simigdalenios)

Serves 20 • Preparation time 5 minutes • Cooking time 15-20 minutes

INGREDIENTS

4-4½ cups water • 2½-3 cups sugar, to taste • 1 cinnamon stick • the rind of one lemon • 6-7 whole cloves • 1 cup melted unsalted butter or vegetable oil • 2 cups coarse semolina • 1/2 cup coarsely chopped almonds or • whole pine nuts • 1/2 teaspoon grated lemon rind

THE GARNISH: cinnamon • 3 oz almonds, blanched and roasted

Follow the package instructions when cooking semolina; the amount of water required will vary according to brand. Put the water and sugar in a large, heavy-bottomed saucepan and stir over medium heat until the sugar is completely dissolved. Add the cinnamon stick, lemon rind, and cloves, cover the pan, and boil the syrup for 5 minutes. Remove the spices; you may substitute vanilla flavoring, if preferred. Heat the butter in a deep, heavy-bottomed pan; add the semolina and brown it over medium heat, stirring constantly until golden. A few minutes before the end of browning, add the almonds. Carefully empty the browned semolina into the hot syrup, stirring constantly. Add the grated lemon rind, and stir the mixture over medium heat until the syrup is absorbed and the semolina is puffed and soft. Halva is ready when it slides off the spoon cleanly. Remove the pan from the heat, cover with a kitchen towel, and replace the lid. Allow to stand for 10-15

minutes; then spoon halva into a large 3-pint mold or into individual jelly molds. Press to pack tightly; then unmold onto a serving dish and sprinkle with a little cinnamon. Garnish with roasted almonds or pine nuts, if desired. Serve warm or cold. Will keep at room temperature up to one week.

Orange Rind Coils

(Rola apo Flouda Portokaliou)

Yields 3 lbs • Preparation time 24 hours • Cooking time 45 minutes

INGREDIENTS

2½ lbs thick skinned oranges • 2 lbs sugar • 2½ cups water • 2 tablespoons lemon juice • 1/2 cup glucose (corn syrup)

Rub the oranges lightly with a fine grater. Score the peel in 4, 6, or 8 segments, according to the size of the fruit, and remove it carefully. Roll each piece tightly, thread on a cotton string, as for a necklace, using a large-eyed needle. Place the coils in a pan, and add water to cover. Let them stand in the water overnight to eliminate the bitterness. The next day put the pan over medium heat, and cook the coils until tender. Slide them off the thread, add the sugar and cook until the syrup is thick. Let them stand in the syrup overnight. The next day, add the lemon juice and glucose and cook until the setting point is reached. While still hot, put the rind coils into sterilized jars and pour the syrup over them. Seal and store in a dark, cool place or preferably in the refrigerator. Follow the same procedure to preserve lemon, Seville orange, bergamot or grapefruit rind coils.

Grated Quince in Syrup

(Kidoni Trifto)

Yields 2 lbs • Preparation time 24 hours • Cooking time 30 minutes

INGREDIENTS

2 lbs quince • 2 tablespoons lemon juice
• 3 cups water • 1½ lbs sugar
• 2 geranium or lemon leaves • 1/2 cup glucose (corn syrup)

Peel the quinces and grate them coarsely to the core over a pan holding the water and lemon juice, so that the fruit falls immediately into the acidulated water, which will prevent discoloration. Put the pan over medium heat. Cover and cook until the fruit is soft and almost all the water has evaporated. Add the sugar and let stand overnight. The next day, simmer over medium heat, stirring frequently for about 15 minutes or until the fruit is soft and translucent and the setting point is reached. Add glucose and geranium leaves 5 minutes before setting. Remove the pan from the heat and let cool. Put in jars, cover, and seal. Stored in a dark, cool place or preferably in the refrigerator, the preserves will keep up to one year.

Easter Sweet Bread

(Tsoureki)

Yields 8 plaited loaves • Preparation time 2 hours • Baking time 20 minutes

INGREDIENTS

7 oz fresh yeast or • 6 tablespoons dry yeast • 1 cup tepid water • 5 lbs bread flour • 3½ cups sugar • 2 teaspoons salt • 2 tablespoons olive oil • 1 tablespoon ground mahlep, or vanilla, or ground mastic, or 4 tablespoons grated citrus rind • 1 teaspoon ground cardamom • 1 cup scalded milk • 10 eggs, at room temperature • 1½ cups warm, melted, unsalted butter • 2 egg yolks beaten with 2 teaspoons water

Mix the yeast with the tepid water in a bowl. Add enough of the flour to form a thick paste. Cover the bowl and leave the mixture in a warm, damp place, until doubled in bulk, about 30 minutes. Put the sugar, salt, oil, and flavorings into a kneading basin. Pour in the scalded milk and stir with a wooden spoon. Break in the eggs; with your fingers, crush the yolks and combine the eggs with the other ingredients. Add and mix in the yeast mixture. Then add the flour in 2-3 stages, working the mixture with your hands until all the flour is moistened, and you have a warm, soft and sticky dough. Using both hands, take handfuls of the melted butter, pour it over the dough, folding and kneading it until all the butter has been incorporated into the dough. Avoid overworking. Traces of butter remaining in the dough will be absorbed as it rises. The dough should be warm, light, and buttery. Cover the basin with greaseproof paper, then wrap it with a blanket. Let the dough rise, until it is three to four times its original bulk, 1-2½ hours. Divide the dough into 18 equal portions. Cover with a kitchen towel. On a floured work surface, shape 3 pieces into long strands and braid them together. Continue shaping and braiding the remaining dough portions, until all of them are used and you have 6 plaited loaves. Place the loaves well apart on greased baking sheets, cover, and leave them in a warm place until doubled in bulk, about 45 minutes. Brush the surface of each loaf with the egg yolk mixture and sprinkle with thinly sliced blanched almonds. Bake in a preheated 400°F oven for about 20 minutes. Avoid overbaking as they dry out quickly. Cool the loaves on wire racks before slicing or storing.